PRAISE FOR

Grandpa's Gift

"This collection of messages is so full of wisdom, encouragement and spiritual insight for today's world you would be forgiven for thinking they were written last month, rather than nearly six decades ago. As someone who has spent much of my life communicating via radio, podcast and video, I know how vital it is to craft a message that hits home within a few short minutes. These thoughts, first delivered on radio in the 1960s, do just that. They are a treasure trove of Christian wisdom that can now be passed on to a new generation. I never knew C. Maxwell Brown, but felt I somehow did by the time I had finished.

The additional thoughts from Dan, as a grandson, bring a delightful personal touch to this collection. It feels as though the spiritual baton is being passed down the generations. Some years ago I had the privilege of recording an extended interview with my own grandfather about his experiences as a POW during World War II which led him to a life of Christian ministry. He passed away soon after, but it remains a meaningful encounter that shapes who I am today. The stories, experiences and wisdom of our forebears must be not be forgotten, but treasured, told and shared anew with each generation. I am so grateful for Dan, for his friendship to me and and for his faithfulness in bringing his own grandfather's humor, love and life lessons to many more people today."

— **JUSTIN BRIERLEY**
    Author, broadcaster and speaker and host of the
    Unbelievable? and *Ask NT Wright Anything* podcasts.
    www.justinbrierley.com

"Dan has been a personal friend and a professional colleague of mine for over twenty years. I was intrigued when I heard he was working on a book to honor the thoughtful wisdom and faith-filled insight of his grandfather. I was moved by the applicability his words from the 1960s have on our society today. My original intent was not necessarily to find a strong faith walk, but this book certainly inspired me to do so!"

— **Bob Sutton**
Chief Executive Officer
Avera Health - Serving South Dakota,
Iowa, Minnesota, and Nebraska

"This book is a joy to read. Dan's authentic voice leaps off of the pages. To learn about Dan's walk toward faith inspired in part by his Grandpa Max's words, stories from so long ago, was a real gift to me!"

— **Marla Meyer**
Chief Executive Officer
Girl Scouts Dakota Horizons
Serving South Dakota, North Dakota,
Western Minnesota, & Northwestern Iowa

"At RESGEN, we are always looking for ways and resources to inspire and help men deepen their relationships with God and others and grow in their Christlikeness in every area of their lives—and we just found another one! In his book, *Grandpa's Gift*, Dan has effectively connected his story of desiring to take his faith more seriously to the timeless wisdom his grandfather shared so many decades ago. I have no doubt this book will inspire everyone who reads it to strengthen their relationships, with both God and others, and serve everyone they are connected to, with a Christ-like love."

— **Tom Henderson**
RESGEN Founder/Speaker
Best-Selling Author and Host of the *RESGEN Giving Life Podcast*

"As a father, a husband, a surgeon, and an entrepreneur who's passionate about the people I serve every day, I'll be encouraging all of them to read this book. Feels like grandpa gave me this 'gift' as an inspired work woven together between a grandson and grandfather. I've known Dan for more than twenty years, and he's touched on something here that's beautiful and available to us all."

— **John Berdahl, MD**
Professor - University of South Dakota
Ophthalmologist, Vance Thompson Vision

"Words of wisdom are timeless, and this book illustrates how relevant the lessons of the past—in this case, from Grandpa Brown – still hold true today. It's an easy read that illustrates the critical importance of keeping one's faith central and living with Christian intentionality through all the ups and downs of life. A great read."

— **Paul TenHaken**
Mayor, Sioux Falls, SD
Christian, Father, Husband, Entrepreneur

"There's an old African proverb that says 'When an old person dies a library burns down.'

In these pages we unlock a library like no other and are transported through time to a world that is so different and so very like our own. I've come to know Dan through our work together at Premier Insight. I am grateful for him and this book, as its stories weave a grandson's walk through his days to the timeless wisdom of his grandfather. This is a book to be savored, not rushed. In it you'll find a wisdom available for us all, at all times. It's amazing what faith can do, and this book may just help us all take it even more seriously."

— **Peter Kerridge**
President & Chief Executive Officer
Premier Christian Communications & Premier Insight
Author, Entrepreneur & Pastor

"After reading this book, I am not surprised that the inspiration for it came from someone with North Dakota roots. 'Grandpa' Brown's messages are informed by nearly thirty years of ministering to the incredibly kind and faithful people of our great state. The message of this text is not only timeless, but it is a reminder that Christ is the source of all joy: past, present, and future.

Although decades have passed and the world has modernized the problems of the times, we can trust that God is present. His love is given freely to us and through us as we lay claim to his message of hope. I thank Dan for republishing this book and for challenging us to BOLDLY say yes when faced with the choice to live simply and freely in the love and promise of Christ."

— **Polly Peterson, PhD**
President, The University of Jamestown
Jamestown, North Dakota

"As I finished reading *Grandpa's Gift*, I was struck by what 'a gift' it is! It's very properly named! The practical wisdom detailed in the spiritual insights Grandpa Max derived from the Word of God and the Holy Spirit apply today and will continue to prove useful for generations to come! I am someone who's spent a career coaching and teaching young adults in sports. As a coach instructs an athlete with patience and support, this book shows how a grandfather can still 'coach' a grandson, even though he left his earthly body more than thirty-five years ago. There is truly something here for everyone, regardless of the season of life in which they find themselves."

— **Tom Goehle**
Assistant Women's Basketball Coach
The University of Nebraska
Former Director, Fellowship of Christian Athletes
& Sports Ambassadors International Ministry

"I was raised in East Palo Alto, California, in the Bay Area! It would have been incredible to have heard Grandpa Max's messages coming in hot over the California radio waves! I am also a follower and servant of Christ Jesus. I am thankful for this book and for the story it tells of a man wrestling in his faith while working to be the best husband, father and business professional he can be. I am striving to do the same in my life, and this book enriched my journey. The lessons are rich with wisdom for this generation and the generation to come! We must keep it moving toward Christ Jesus!"

#K.I.M. #OneGod #Bsheku #GrandpaMax

> — **SHEKU BANNISTER**
> Market Executive, Midco
> Civil Rights Commissioner, Musician, Writer, CEO of Survival Records
> Founder of K.I.M. - Keep It Moving

"Dan has done a masterful job of combining his grandfather's sermons from over fifty years ago, with his own faith walk. Including the struggles, perseverance and final victory that comes when we encounter Christ, we begin to see the world and our neighbors through the eyes of God.

Without question, the biblical principles that Dan and his grandfather unpack in this book are absolutely God's roadmap."

> — **TODD KNUTSON**
> Author *The Kingdom Force*
> Vice President of Advancement
> The University of Sioux Falls

"At Throne, we've published more than 450 books for authors all over the world. I am always excited to see an author's project come to life, and I am often really inspired by their books. But, this one, THIS one, has really moved me, and I know it will move you, too. Dan takes us on a grandson's journey to an intentional, bold and ultimately new life-giving response to Jesus' call for all of us. His Grandpa Maxwell's faith-filled wisdom from the early 1960s helped him get there, and I hope it helps you, too.

I'll never forget when Dan first showed me the book and, as I read Maxwell's words from decades ago, realized how relevant to today they are.

I'm so grateful for Dan taking the time to add his commentary and thoughts, which add incredible value and perspective to his grandfather's timeless wisdom!"

— **Jeremy Brown**
Founder & Chief Executive Officer
Throne Publishing Group

"As a believer and a leader of people from all kinds of experiences and backgrounds, I am grateful for this book. The story weaves a grandson's walk toward a higher calling in this life to the timeless wisdom of his grandfather. It's a wisdom available for us all, at all times. It's amazing what an active and intentional faith can do. This book may help us all be more intentional with our life, our actions and our habits. These messages from another season in American history are relevant and inspiring for today. My prayer is you would be drawn nearer to and see Jesus more clearly as you enjoy this work."

— **Ross Allen**
President, Bethel University
Retired Medtronic Executive

"I hired Dan nearly twenty years ago … at the conclusion of our introductory lunch, my offer to him was scribbled on the back of a napkin. This book shows a deeper side of him that I instinctively knew was there. I'm so pleased that he has undertaken this journey to share what drives his decision-making every day. It's apparent to our associates, customers and vendors that Dan walks the talk, and that's refreshing in these times. I hope you will enjoy these timeless, relatable stories and the remarkable interplay between grandfather and grandson. It's worth your time."

— **John H. Nelson**
CEO & Chairman
HUB International - Great Plains

"This book touched my heart. To learn about Dan's intentional steps, made clearer by his grandfather's lessons from long ago, gradually leading him toward a strong faith was a real gift to me and I believe it will be to so many others! I'm excited to be a partner with Rock Ranch in the ministry of hope & healing for all."

— **Lynn Moore**
Founder & CEO
Acres for Life - Therapy & Wellness Center
www.acresforlife.org

GRANDPA'S GIFT

GRANDPA'S GIFT

How Old Wisdom Can Inspire New Life

Dan LaRock

WITH C. Maxwell Brown

THRONE
PUBLISHING GROUP

Copyright © 2022 by Dan LaRock

ISBN Softcover: 979-8-88739-037-6
ISBN Hardcover: 979-8-88739-036-9
Ebook ISBN: 979-8-88739-038-3

All rights reserved. No part of this book may be reproduced or transmitted in any form or by any means, electronic or mechanical, including photocopying, recording or by any information storage and retrieval system, without permission in writing from the copyright owner. For information on distribution rights, royalties, derivative works or licensing opportunities on behalf of this content or work, please contact the publisher at the address below.

"Scripture quotations marked (ESV) are from The ESV® Bible (The Holy Bible, English Standard Version®), copyright © 2001 by Crossway, a publishing ministry of Good News Publishers. Used by permission. All rights reserved."

Scriptures taken from the Holy Bible, New International Version®, NIV®. Copyright © 1973, 1978, 1984, 2011 by Biblica, Inc.™ Used by permission of Zondervan. All rights reserved worldwide. www.zondervan.com The "NIV" and "New International Version" are trademarks registered in the United States Patent and Trademark Office by Biblica, Inc.™

Scripture quotations from The Authorized (King James) Version. Rights in the Authorized Version in the United Kingdom are vested in the Crown. Reproduced by permission of the Crown's patentee, Cambridge University Press

Scripture marked NKJV is taken from the New King James Version®. Copyright © 1982 by Thomas Nelson. Used by permission. All rights reserved.

Although the author and publisher have made every effort to ensure that the information and advice in this book were correct and accurate at press time, the author and publisher do not assume and hereby disclaim any liability to any party for any loss, damage, or disruption caused from acting upon the information in this book or by errors or omissions, whether such errors or omissions result from negligence, accident, or any other cause.

Printed in the United States of America.

Throne Publishing Group
1601 East 69th St N Suite 306
Sioux Falls, SD 57108
ThronePG.com

ANY PROCEEDS GENERATED BY GRANDPA'S GIFT

Should there be proceeds produced by sales of this book, they will be used to help further the mission and ministry of Rock Ranch located in Martin Township near Hills, Minnesota.

My wife, Marie, listened for years to the calling of the Holy Spirit with respect to how we should best use the gifts God gave us. I can't help but look at Grandpa Max's lesson "The God Who Intervenes" as a perfect example of how this organization came into being and has since been blessed by His hand. Marie has been gifted this opportunity to reach thousands for Jesus, and I am so thankful to be at her side helping support this work.

Together, through Rock Ranch, we are simply and (Lord willing) dutifully trying to answer that call, the whispers of the Holy Spirit to help share His love with children, seniors and all people in need through the art and skills of horsemanship.

For more about Rock Ranch, please feel free to visit: www.RideRockRanch.org or search #riderockranch on Facebook, Instagram or LinkedIn.

ROCK RANCH
Est. 2016
www.riderockranch.org

Table of Contents

Foreword . . . . *xix*
About Grandpa's Gift. xxi

COLLECTION ONE 1
    Give the World "The Heisman" 3
    Finding God in Our Daily Contacts 5
    Character Is Costly 11
    El Camino Real 17
    Thoughts on Collection One 23

COLLECTION TWO 27
    Be Bold. Watch What Happens. 29
    I Was a Stranger. 30
    The Way of Habits That Help 36
    The Way of Drift or Decision 42
    Thoughts on Collection Two 48

COLLECTION THREE 53
    Intentional Love in All Relationships 55
    Childhood's Bill of Rights 58
    For the Loneliness that Desolates Us 64
    For the Joys that Invite Us 70
    Thoughts on Collection Three 75

COLLECTION FOUR 79
    Oh No! History Matters?! 81
    You Can Find God in History 83
    The Greatest Story Ever Told 89
    The God Who Intervenes 94
    Thoughts on Collection Four 101

COLLECTION FIVE 105
    What About the Future? 107
    For The Guilt That Haunts Us 108
    God Commands – But Gently 114
    Hope Springs Eternal 119
    Thoughts on Collection Five 125

Final Thoughts 129
What Feeds My Brain? 133

Endnotes *137*
About the Author *141*

*This book seeks to honor the lifework of
my grandfather, C. Maxwell Brown.*

*I thank GOD every day for
Marie, Zach, Luke & The Gator.*

*In honor of my earthly father, James Delano LaRock,
who passed in March 2022.*

"Live for the applause of nail scarred hands."
— Mark Batterson, Chase the Lion

Foreword

I'm given a lot of books. A lot!

Daily they come in the mail from different publishers. Regularly someone will give me a copy of this or that book.

More often than not, I kindly take the book, go to my office, and put it on my shelf—never to be read.

When my friend, Dan, handed me a bland (boring) covered copy of his grandfather's book, the chances of me ever opening it were honestly slim to none.

But due to my respect for Dan and my love for words that weren't written yesterday (I'd argue the true sign of a good book is one with words that still ring true years, or even decades, later), I surprisingly took the book home with me.

It sat on my nightstand for a week or so and then one night I opened it.

And for several weeks in a row, I found myself opening the book each night before going to sleep.

I couldn't put it down.

The words inside were filled with grace and wisdom.

It felt like I was sitting down with a wise, older mentor teaching me about God and life.

But what struck me most was the timeliness of Dan's grandfather's words. Even as I write this, I still can't believe how relevant they are.

Paragraph after paragraph, chapter after chapter felt like it was written yesterday—meant to address something our world (and me personally) is wrestling with today.

Once I finished the book, I couldn't speak with Dan fast enough.

"Your grandfather's book is unbelievably good," I told him.

"You think so?" he asked.

In an effort to not come off as rude, I didn't tell him that my first thought when he handed me the book was that I would never read it. Instead, I told Dan what I knew to be true after reading his grandfather's words: how what he wrote had impacted me profoundly and how I knew those words would do the same for others.

I'm delighted Dan decided to share the words of his grandfather with you, too.

I only hope what he wrote will impact you, like it did me.

ADAM WEBER
Lead pastor of Embrace Church
Author of *Talking With God* and *Love Has a Name*
Host of *The Conversation* Podcast

About Grandpa's Gift

My dream for this book is to celebrate the timeless thoughts and words of my grandfather, C. Maxwell Brown. Grandpa was a pastor, born in South Dakota, ministering to congregations in North Dakota and across the country from the 1920s into the early '60s. He began working more than a hundred years ago.

When Grandpa moved to California, he wrote and delivered radio addresses in the Oakland / San Francisco Bay Area. Those messages were collected by my maternal grandmother, Dorothy, (who passed in 1972) and then brought back to life in the 1980s by his second wife, Evelyn, in a self-published book, *Backpacking in a Cultural Wilderness*.

Widely distributed in the Bay Area, the book did find its way across the country eventually but was never formally published or backed by an actual publishing house. In my quest to find the remaining copies a number of years ago, I was pleasantly surprised to discover them on Amazon in independent bookstores across the country. I bought as many of them as I could find.

I wanted to read the book again, in many ways for the first time, and I am very happy I did. I am so energized by its content. I am so calmed by its delivery. I sit in humble appreciation of the work. I am awestruck by its timeliness for the world we live in today. I think it has something for everyone, especially busy people looking for answers. That was me. I needed this book, for so many reasons. It's become *Grandpa's Gift* to me. For everyone.

The messages were written and delivered between 1963 and 1965. For those in tune with U.S. history, you'll know that these are a few of the more tumultuous years in our country's existence. Racial tensions. Class wars. Governmental challenges. Youth disillusionment. It's all in there, and it's all very real. Yesterday and today.

My grandfather's messages were inspired by more than forty years of ministering to the people of the Dakotas, but his thoughts are far from geographically or culturally isolated. To me, they're incredibly insightful. Born from his patient work on behalf of Jesus Christ.

As I have read and re-read his book, many thoughts spring to mind.

The first is from Ecclesiastes 1:9: "What has been is what will be, and what has been done is what will be done, and there is nothing new under the sun" (ESV).

The next comes from a little more secular source:

"Don't throw the past away
You might need it some rainy day
Dreams can come true again
When everything old is new again"

Those are the lyrics from the iconic song, "Everything Old is New Again," by Carole Sager and Peter Allen.[1]

There are words here for everyone. Anyone. New believers. Established Christians. Those most devout. And those still searching for eternal answers.

My true hope is that my grandfather's words of more than fifty years ago will help people see the things happening today are not new, they've existed before. There have been tough times. People have struggled. Racial tensions are real. Teens rebel. Governments underwhelm us. People search for meaning. Sometimes they find it. Sometimes … well … that's the point.

I believe my grandfather laid out a path for all of us. It's a familiar one to many. Foreign to many as well. It's the path of Jesus. It's the Way of the Bible. It's Christianity.

About Grandpa's Gift

I believe if we want the world fifty years from now to look differently than it does today, we all need Jesus. The real Jesus—born and raised in the Middle East. Jewish. Learned. Patient. Kind. Forgiving. Today, followed by more than two billion of us. His way is the Way of God. And, I am finally seeing now, at fifty-two. His is a good way. A noble, peaceful path. A way to navigate our world. Its people. Its problems. All of it.

I hope, I pray, you'll take the time to read this book, to celebrate the lifework of someone I only knew through my early teen years, but I'm coming to know better and better every day, through his timeless words.

I'm going to share a little over half of the messages from *"Backpacking"* with you. I ask for your patience as I introduce each collection of messages with a few of my thoughts and stories. I have *italicized* certain sections of Grandpa's messages as those parts spoke to me as important throughout my time in his book. I hope they add color and help us all see the timelessness of Grandpa's words. My faith in Jesus has been in construction for some time. My path was not suddenly altered by *Backpacking in a Cultural Wilderness*, but it was, in many ways, cemented.

I hope we can learn from the wisdom shared through these historical messages. If we can, then maybe we will not be doomed to dismay over the personal and societal ills of the future. Perhaps today, we can read and understand the medicinal regimen prescribed in my grandfather's words, apply it to the world around us today, and pray for a future in which these challenges are, more often than not, in our collective rearview mirrors.

There is a story here. I'll try to keep it brief and, Lord willing, interesting. I'm so thankful you're considering reading this book. My true hope is that you, too, can find Grandpa's Gift.

Just "a Bit" About Me (Dan)

My truest desire for what you're about to read is that the words of my grandfather, C. Maxwell Brown, will somehow strike you as life-giving, even essential reading for these times in which we are now living.

Backpacking In a Cultural Wilderness was first written in 1985. I was fifteen, and while the idea of a book coming out of our family tree was cool, its subject being a collection of sermons preached in the '60s provided very little interest for me.

Sermons were for Sundays, not for daily digestion.

I was far more interested in the latest John Mellencamp, U2, or Van Halen albums than a book about God, even if my grandfather had written it.

To paraphrase a U2 song, I still hadn't really found what I was looking for. In fact, I wasn't even sure what I was looking for.

I did read it though. Well, ten pages or so, and then, after about a week, I put it away. At least I could say I had *tried* to read it.

I dusted off the book around my twenty-first birthday. I was in college, but again found it hard to read amidst the multitude of social and worldly experiences, fraternity life, Coors Light and the pursuit of numerous other distractions, many of them awesome, sometimes regrettable, but awesome nonetheless!

Still, I was not in the frame of mind with God to appreciate "*Backpacking.*" Sorry, Grandpa.

Ultimately, I wound up 0 for 2.

College did produce a home run for me though; her name was Marie Elizabeth Nelson, now Marie LaRock. And while that's also an incredible story, it's not what this book is all about. However, we were married in 1994 and began working on life, chasing the American dream. We caught it, too. At least as the world describes it.

Some of the best parts came into being in 2000 and 2003. Their names are Luke James and Allie Marie (The Gator). We also welcomed another member into our home in 2011, Zach Allen. He's awesome. And our family became five. Again, they are not what this book is about, *but* they are some of the biggest reasons I am chasing what this book is about.

If you had asked me about my faith around the year 2000, I likely would have told you I'd been in "God's Camp" for much of my life. Albeit, I was hanging out in the back, even asleep in the pews a few times.

Around the age of thirty-five, I began to become more interested. I'm sure it was a move in me as a father, trying to be better for Marie, for our kids, for my family. It was about then, 2006 or so, that I accepted an invitation to a Christian overnight event called a "Cursillo," where I had a very close encounter of the "difficult-to-explain" kind, while becoming more immersed into a Christian walk.

Then I watched Mel Gibson's *The Passion of The Christ* and became even more interested in history. Which, strangely enough, I've come to see in a lot of ways as "His-Story." I became more involved at church, more curious, even more convicted.

And the music. The music again. I started listening, hearing the messages. Hearing the stories. Van Halen plays became fewer while Casting Crowns became more prominent in the rotation. John Mellencamp was still on my list, but Third Day and NEEDTOBREATHE were moving up the charts.

For the next ten years or so, I was involved in a different kind of chase. Looking for a different kind of prize. "Bettering" myself, wrapped in a Christian bow, feeling good about success in the race I was running. During this time, my career was truly taking off, and I had a lot going on, business wise.

The "freedom" found in financial independence is really appealing. It is a goal so many people pursue, some for their entire lives. I can't pretend it's not worthwhile. I won't pretend it's not attractive. When achieved, it does provide a certain kind of worldly security.

According to every Google search engine result available, and in the opinion of our financial advisor and most banks, the "world" would define my family's financial position as being in the top two percent but not quite the one percent. In my simple mind, that appears to be a 98 percent grade, an academic "A".

I won't shrug it off.

It took a lot of work to make it happen. It also took some luck. But here is what I honestly and truly do know.

It will never be enough.

It will never satisfy.

The more I have, the more the world tells me I need.

There's always an upgrade. Always a platinum service. A bigger screen. More pixels. More thread counts. A better seat on the plane. First-class for, well, anything and everything. A more comfortable vehicle. A bigger boat.

A closer view of the ocean, the mountains, the river, the ... whatever. There will always be something more money can buy.

And it will never be enough.

That realization a number of years ago left me searching. It left me looking for deeper meaning in my relationships and in our world. We had so much "comfort," so much goodness in our marriage and in our family, but for some reason I was not 100 percent content with my life. With the direction I needed to head.

Around 2015, when I read these words from Grandpa's book, I realized he'd discovered something I was looking for, and they shook me:

> In Jesus of Nazareth, we firmly believe that God intervened in human history by giving us, in human form, a definition of His own Spirit, a delineation of His hopes for mankind, an invitation to step up to a new level of personal and social living. And since we know about Him, we cannot avoid doing something about Him. Whether we follow Him or deliberately ignore Him, God has intervened in our lives by requiring us to choose.

"Requiring?!?!"

Oh boy. That's rough. That's not how I've been wanting it to be. That's not what I've been practicing.

Have I been drinking "Christian Lite" all these years?

What do I do now?

For the first time, my head and heart began to align toward Him. And at the very core of my being, I realized Grandpa Max was right.

My prayer is that this book will in some small way push you to *"choose"* life more fully in pursuit of His goodness. Do your research. Spend time in the Bible. Read it. Read it again. Step out of your chase for worldly success and step into His calling for all of us. If you do, I truly believe you'll understand and see it with your own eyes.

It's an incredible thing to see. Hard to describe.

I think it's like seeing ...

... Joy.

With no filters.
With no glasses.
Simply "unfiltered Joy."

Here's how I've come to see it and continue to learn more about it, with Grandpa's help. I'll lay it out in five collections moving forward. Each new part will include a bit of preview from me and then a few messages from my grandfather, circa the mid-1960's.

Even though some of his thoughts clearly reveal the world he was living in with respect to human traditions and family roles, I've been able to set those aside and not let them distract me from the good stuff. It's been incredible for me to read his words and realize how clearly the solution for what ails us in so many areas is simply woven, even grafted, into our society. It has been here for centuries, twenty or so of them. We've just covered it up.

I hope these next pages provide you a reason to uncover it, rediscover it, or even find it for the first time. It's changed the game for me and for my family. The first collection is called: Give the World "The Heisman."

And it begins right now.

COLLECTION ONE

Give the World "The Heisman"

Since 1935, The Heisman Memorial Trophy has been awarded annually to the most outstanding player in college football. Winners have typically moved on from college to enjoy successful professional careers either as players, coaches, or business leaders, often a combination of all three.

The trophy is well-recognized in the world of sports. It features a leather helmeted player carrying a leather football in one arm, his second arm extended, ready to push an opponent out of his way and continue to move the ball forward.

The second, extended arm is frequently referred to as a "stiff-arm." When used properly, it keeps opponents at bay, forcing them to deal with more than just a runner while making an attempted tackle. The "stiff-arm" is a weapon the skilled player uses to advance down the field of play by keeping those who would distract, deter, and otherwise take him down, at bay.

The move has come to be known in some circles simply as "The Heisman." I've heard it used to describe numerous kinds of situations, some wholly unrelated to football.

For example, picture a city park. People are going about their days. There are children with their parents. Pets and bikes and small groups of friends are gathered together, talking. In one of those groups, a young woman "rejects" a forward advance from a young man. It would not surprise me in the least to hear someone in that group provide this observation: "She gave him The Heisman!"

Situations where people push distractions out of their paths of progress, shove aside the things which slow them down or even stop them altogether from moving forward, are potential opportunities to use "The Heisman."

Here are other areas I now believe need to receive "The Heisman":

Climbing the ladder.

The ways of the world.

The chase for success.

The pursuit of relevance.

Making it in America.

All of these are ideas I've believed in at one point in my life, maybe even at several points in my life. They describe goals I've pursued. I've actually "caught" each of them, held them in my hands at different times, spent time with them, and looked to each for meaning.

To this day, I've not found it in any of those things. And I know I won't find it there. It has to be found in another way, a simpler way, a more natural way that leads to pure joy. It starts by pushing aside the things which distract and deter us from riding that rhythm in this world. Giving the world "The Heisman." Here's are few messages my grandfather read over the California airwaves nearly sixty years ago. See how they hit today.

Finding God in Our Daily Contacts

December 13, 1964

In Aldous Huxley's novel *Brave New World*, we have a picture of our world organized as it might well be in the not-too-distant future. A mechanized, automated world, drained dry of human sentiment, perhaps, but running smoothly as a well-oiled and well-balanced machine. One of the officers in this engineered world is discussing matters with a colleague who still retained some remnants of religious faith, a holdover from pre-scientific ages. The holdover said, "Then you think there is no God?" "No," answered the dictator, "I think there quite probably is one. But he manifests himself in different ways to different men. In pre-modern days he manifested himself in ways described in these books," and he indicated the *Holy Bible* and William James' *The Varieties of Religious Experience*. Replied the first man, "Then how does he manifest himself now?" "Well," came the reply, "he manifests himself now as an absence; as though he weren't there at all."

And this of course is as it seems to many living in our time. *The wherewithal of rather abundant material life seems always at hand, not through the providence of God, but rather the skill of an organization or of a human effort. Many moderns never get close enough to nature to marvel at that which no man ever has been able to reproduce—the color, form and fragrance of a single rose petal, or the miracle of a hundred kernels of wheat from one small seed. They do not find God anywhere because they do not look for Him anywhere.*

Though the Bible is still a best seller, it is questionable how many read it with understanding of its message. It's the story of God and man in living relationship. We spoke last week of finding God in the reading of the Bible, and so we may. But among other things, the Bible would teach us that we ought also to find God in our day-by-day relationships of life, for this is where they who wrote the book found Him. Theodore Gill, in an article on the nature of the Biblical story, reminds us of what we are likely to forget, that the Biblical writers were not primarily philosophers, poets, or literary men at all. They were carpenters, farmers, shepherds, and merchantmen involved in the daily business of making a living and making a life. They were not folk on vacation writing back to their friends, "We are having a wonderful time; wish you were here." They were people involved in the hard daily grind, in this sordid, bitter, and often disappointing world, writing of what they really experienced, and it goes like this, "Having a terrible time; glad God is here." Just so, if we will, we can look for and find the Divine Presence in the very human present of our daily lives.

We must remember that God is Spirit, and as Jesus reminded us, the Spirit, as the wind, is observed only by what it does with clouds and trees and waves and snow. The Spirit of God moving the spirits of men in turn moves men to act, and it is in their acts that we see the power of God disclosed. The Biblical idea of God is as spirit which brings order out of chaos. Under the Spirit's creative influence, chaos became the cosmos. So, we may expect to find God active in any situation when disorder is transformed to order. So, the busy housewife, who, despite family confusion, does her best to restore a semblance of orderliness, is God's handmaiden, doing His work and His will. Just so with the legislator, working long hours in committee, studying the needs of his community, finding, often through compromise, a workable solution to conflicts. He, too, will be doing the will of God and thus revealing the work of God by helping the family of man to live together in harmony and mutual helpfulness. I can see no reason why we cannot say and mean it, that the traffic officer standing at the intersection of busy streets to keep the flow of human life on its purposeful way is providing some "divine guidance" for the children of God. God is the Spirit of Order. But also the Creative Spirit, who takes the component parts and creates a thing of beauty or utility—a tree, a mountain, a man. In less spectacular ways, but just as real, this Creative Spirit of God moves through human spirits, to build houses and cathedrals, to paint pictures, and plan cities, to invent machines and compose symphonies. It is the Creative Spirit of the Creative God which moves men to create something new, a thing of beauty or utility, an expression of that within man which demands translation into reality. For this reason, men employed the best of the creative arts—architecture, music, poetry, drama—to express their devotion to the God of Creative Power.

But God is also the Spirit of Truth, that in man which responds to the truth, hungers for the truth, and will even willingly die for the truth. To me, a school room is as sacred a place as a church, for here, little children come to know God who is Truth spelled out in great and simple formulae. A child who learned that two plus two equals four has had an experience with eternity. He has grasped something as valid and real as if he had felt the touch of Jesus' hand on his head, Jesus who said of himself, "I am the Truth." To my mind, a dedicated schoolteacher is a prophet of the most high, a servant of God, in the service of man. It is an interesting footnote to history that the first schools were also the synagogue, the house of worship. *There are those in our land who are greatly disturbed because compulsory prayer is not practiced in our schools. They assume, I suspect, that God does not arrive at school unless someone invites Him through prayer.* Have we forgotten that Jesus taught us that, "Ye shall know the truth, and the truth shall set you free"? Truth is the greatest emancipator, it is the servant of God, setting the minds and spirits of men free to possess the world, to use its powers, and to order their own lives with reverence and mutual respect. You will find God present wherever men are seeking to know the truth. I remember seeing a laboratory scene on television where men were conducting experiments to discover more of the secrets of nature. A sign read, "All who enter here must wear a sterile gown and mask." They might have added with equal relevance, "Remove your shoes for you are standing on holy ground."

It is the Christian's insistence that God is also the Spirit of Love. For this reason, the Cross, on which our Master willingly died as an act designed to win men to Himself and through Him to the God of love, is our foremost symbol. It surmounts our church steeples and is the central focus of worship in all Christian churches. The Epistle of John says it this way, "And we have seen and testify that the Father has sent his Son to be the Savior of the world. If anyone acknowledges that Jesus is the Son of God, God lives in them and they in God. And so we know and rely on the love God has for us. God is love. Whoever lives in love lives in God, and God in them." Jacques Maritain, French scholar and theologian, reminds us that every experience of love is an experience of God, for God is love.

If this is true, and I for one am confident it is, then we encounter God daily as we see love in action, on our streets, in our homes, throughout our community and world.

We visited a home the other day where a young couple was proudly showing us their first child, a boy of two weeks. Watching the little mother handle this babe with loving concern, one knew instinctively that here was a sacred place, and this a sacred moment. Here was love, through which a new life had come into the world, continuing to be expressed in word and gesture and constant care. The Church has made marriage a sacred relationship because it saw in the creative relationship of love the power of God expressed. For this same reason it administers the sacrament of baptism to infants to bring the love of the church family to share in the nurture and guidance of this child of God's love.

But the divine love acts in human affairs far beyond the precincts of home and nursery. It moves out through the dedicated and love-inspired lives of millions of God's children who work for the well-being of the human race. The Bible relates the healing miracles of Jesus, how He opened the eyes of the blind. And those who saw it, were sure that God was present. And indeed, He was, but also present in that operating room where a skilled physician removes the scales of cataract growth from an aged saint's eyes, and she who was blind now sees. I see it constantly in my work as pastor visiting the hospitals. Jesus unstopped deaf ears, and the deaf could hear. Because men care, they are opening the ears of millions these days to hear again the song of the bird, and the voice of love, and the chords of great music. Jesus said of his work, "Greater things than these shall you do, because I go to my Father," and going, He shared His spirit of love with the world. Since that day long ago, hospitals have sprung up to give comfort and bring healing to the sick bodies all over the world. *We must never forget that the hospital, as the school, came into being because the God of Truth, who is also the God of Love, became known to men through the teaching and healing of Jesus of Nazareth.* And through these institutions, the spiritual offspring of the healing Christ, the Spirit which moved and empowered Him still moves and empowers men and women to restore health and happiness to the sick. I see God at work each time I enter a hospital door.

We read the story of Christ feeding the multitude and say, here indeed is proof of God's presence and power. I saw God feeding still greater multitudes just days ago. Across America, during the recent Thanksgiving observance, millions of American believers in God and servants of God became His hands and feet and heart in sending millions of tons of surplus food to starving people across the seas. It is called the SOS program, "Share Our Surplus," by which money, given voluntarily, is used to pay the shipping costs of surplus food stored in America's bursting granaries. As I watched worshippers in the church I serve placing their gifts on the offering plate, I saw again in my mind's eye the Son of God, still moved with compassion, feeding the hungry. And I think of missionaries, trained agriculturists, and Peace Corpsmen, leaving home and comfort to teach the unlearned the secret of making two stalks of corn grow where one grew before, and I know God is still among men feeding the hungry, healing the sick.

Just now I am sharing with a group of citizens a study of critical problems of unemployment in our American life. I find there a room full of people, paying money out of their own pockets to seek, under trained leadership, an answer to the condition in our society which is destroying millions of people, destroying them inwardly, crushing their spirits. *For the young man and young woman who can find nowhere to earn his living, soon loses any sense of his own worth and, robbed of incentive, deteriorates in his own eyes as well as the eyes of others.* These folks go to this trouble, not because they must, but because they care. Moved by a compassion, a feeling with and for the unfortunate, they sacrifice their time and money and energy to find an answer. I find God there, expressed as love become practical community planning. I wonder where we think God ought to be found. Only in church buildings? Only in books? We are about to celebrate the birth of Jesus. We call it the "incarnation"—God in the flesh. God moving out into the street and stores and factories and schools and legislative halls and hospitals, moving everywhere when His children struggle for a life of meaning and happiness. We go to the church to hear His word. We go out of the church to find Him at work among men. Yes, you can find God on your street if you look there for Him.

Character Is Costly

March 7, 1965

"... Your name shall no longer be called Jacob, but Israel, for you have striven with God and men, and have prevailed." Genesis 32:28 (ESV)

Any intelligent man who sets out to build a house will do two things. He will adopt a plan and then compute the cost. Any intelligent man will do the same in building his own life. Any other procedure means disappointment and perhaps disaster. All of us have seen houses that just seem to have happened, architectural monstrosities, housekeepers' nightmares. I remember living in such a parsonage at one time. It appeared that each time a new baby arrived in the family, a room was added to the house. And ministers had large families back in those early days! All of us have seen personalities, perhaps even by looking into a mirror, which appear as angular and as ugly as that house. They represent a series of unplanned adaptations to changing circumstance.

But more than a plan is necessary. A wise man will count the cost of building. For many years between 1930 and 1950, anyone visiting the city of Minot, North Dakota would see what we had come to call "Sparrow Hotel." Just as the depression struck, a corporation began the erection of a large hotel. But they underestimated the cost, and there, for a couple of decades, stood a bare steel frame occupied only by sparrows which built their nests along the girders. It has since been completed; I am glad to report. In building a life, there are costs to be paid. Most of us, I suspect, can find incomplete areas of our own lives, the person we dreamed of becoming, unrealized, just because we were unwilling to pay the price. Yes, the plan and the price are both essential to building either a castle or a character.

I know of no textbook on character-building quite so famous, and properly so, as the Book of Life, the Holy Bible. One finds in its pages all types of characters, good, bad, and indifferent, together with the blueprints and the cost estimates. There are no hidden costs, and the specifications are clear for all to read. Let's look at just one today, a rare person, who in himself illustrates both failure and success. His name is Jacob. I chose him because, in his failure and his success, he seems to speak directly to our condition, we who suffer a degree of failure while we cling to high hopes of something better.

Jacob was the second born of twin sons of Isaac and Rebekah. The story has it that he was born grasping the heel of his brother, so he was given the name "Jacob" which means "heel grasper" or one who trips another. And he became that kind of person. His brother, Esau, was physically strong, athletic, a hunter. Jacob was the smaller, less active of the two. Isaac, the father, doted on his athletic son, while Jacob was his mother's favorite, who doubtless spoiled him with her attention and planned with him to outwit his bigger but slower-witted brother.

One day Esau returned from hunting, famished, and Jacob capitalized on his hunger to trade him a bit of food for Esau's place as leader of the clan. Later, with his mother's collaboration, he disguised himself and approached his father, now blind from age, and received the patriarch's blessing as clan leader. Through both these devious acts, Jacob stood to gain both power and wealth. He was a conscienceless crook and exploiter of others' weaknesses.

But he was not to get away with it all scot-free. Esau turned on his brother who was forced to run for his life. His mother sent him to live with her brother, in another neighborhood far removed. But Uncle Laban was Rebekah's brother in character as in fact he took every advantage of this younger (family member) now dependent upon him. Jacob fell in love with Rachel, Laban's younger daughter, a beautiful girl. Laban made a deal with Jacob: marriage to Rachel in return for seven years labor. When the time came for the marriage to take place, however, Laban substituted an older and plainer daughter under the bridal veil, and Jacob found himself married to Leah. We will have to give him credit for determination, for when Laban said, "Seven more years at hard labor for Rachel," Jacob agreed, and the story goes on, "So great was his love for her that the seven years were but days to him." So, fourteen years of hard labor later, he had his Rachel. But this was not the end of it all. Jacob was still Jacob, the heel grasper. As chief shepherd of the flocks, he was paid in kind. All sheep of a certain color were to be his, so during mating season Jacob arranged that the proper animals mated and became richer and richer at Laban's expense. This was hardly calculated to win the father-in-law's affection, and Jacob was driven out again. So, taking his wives, his flocks, his treasures, and some of Laban's, too, he stole away at night, turning toward his homeland, hoping to find asylum there. But as he approached his brother's domain, the fear of his brother's anger returned. Then came the crisis in Jacob's life.

According to the story, Jacob stole away from camp one night and spent the night alone, "struggling with an adversary." We might say he was struggling with his conscience. In fact, he met that night with God, wrestling with the high standard of His ethical demands, and came out of the encounter a new man. And his new character was indicated in a new name… no longer was he to be Jacob, a tripper of others, but Israel, which means a Prince, for God said, "You have striven with God and men and have prevailed." From one who made his way in life by deception and exploitation, Jacob became the servant of the Highest, and the founder of the new nation, the nation which bears his name, Israel. It is a fascinating story, but what does it say to us? Let me indicate a few facts which are applicable to you and to me, and everyone who is interested in the business of building a life.

First, it says this. *All of us are in a very real sense responsible for what we become.* To be sure, there is heritage, something to be dealt with. Jacob was born a "heel grasper." Here was family influence, a doting parent adding to his character weakness. In our day, we are inclined to stop right here and say, "You see, I can't help being what I am. I was born This Way and my parents made me what I am." I am sorry to say that we have moved from what can be a helpful understanding of our personal peculiarities or biases to a point where we are too ready to assume no responsibility for what we are or what we become. I remember Charlie Brown, in the *Peanuts* comic strip, who one day tipped a vase and broke it. His little friend gleefully accused him, reminding him that he must take responsibility for it. Charlie replied with what in some quarters is acceptable wisdom, "Maybe I can blame it on society." *But it is time we discovered that we are not helpless victims of our heritage nor the circumstances of our upbringing.* Jacob chose from several possibilities in his life, a pattern represented by devotion to God as ethical righteousness. He wrestled with his adversary and came out a different man. There was a plan to challenge him and a price to pay.

The story has another clue for us who are concerned with becoming something, or somebody. It is this. All character is costly, be it good strong character, or weak ineffectual character. Dr. Harry Emerson Fosdick many years ago asserted this with unforgettable clarity when he reminded us that there are no bargain counters in life. He said, "Take what you want and pay for it." There are no handouts here.

We have to pay sometime, somehow. The easy, undisciplined, effortless life may seem to be a bargain. One takes it a day at a time, with the least possible effort. But this is the "live-now pay-later" plan, and, like all delayed payments, it is mighty costly. For the lad or lass who refuses to practice costly self-discipline pays all his or her life for underdeveloped skills and opportunities missed or never offered. This is the sad plight of the "school drop-out" who, taking the cheap and easy way, discovered it is truly the hardest way and the costliest way. On the other hand, we can pay "cash," so to speak, paying the price as we go for the person we want to be today and tomorrow. We find it will pay dividends throughout a lifetime. *Jacob, you see, took the path of least resistance at first, sponging off his brother, rejecting all family responsibility in pursuit of his own self-interest. But he paid in terms of broken home relations. He found no place he could call his own. A cheater, he found himself cheated at every turn.* One is reminded of the words of Jesus,

"Enter the straight gate, for straight is the gate and narrow the way that leads to life"—straight meaning a disciplined, prepared life. "But broad is the way," said He, "that leads to death, and many go in thereat."

A study of any great personality shows the same choice to be faced. Jesus made it in the desert of temptation when He chose to serve God and Him only, turning His back on an easier and, at the moment, very attractive alternative. Saul became Paul, at a great cost to himself. On one occasion, recounting his standing as a young Pharisee, he said, "I counted it all as nothing in choosing to serve Christ as Lord." It cost Martin Luther a high price to spearhead a religious revolution. But he paid that price to become the Father of the Reformation.

Florence Nightingale paid with the abandonment of her life of wealth and ease to enter what, in her time, was a despised profession, nursing. But she became the idol of millions who later followed her impassive service to the sick of mankind. Just so Becket, having to choose the easier life of service to his King, or stand loyally for God, paid the price, and left the world in his debt. These all glimpsed a plan that challenged them and paid the price to build on that plan.

It is no accident that, in every case, the individual made his choice in an encounter with God. Jacob could exclaim, "I have met God face to face and my life is saved." For the plan of life for mankind is found in every man's capacity for high ethical and moral behavior, the pattern discovered in man's encounter with God. Is not this another way of saying that we are never fully human until we have moved up in response to the call of the God of righteousness? Jacob's new chapter developed from this new vision, new image of himself as he stood before God, and his obedience to that vision. The stranger who represented God said, "You are a new man, no longer Jacob the heel grasper, but Israel the Prince, for you have striven with God and man and have prevailed." And that is the secret, the vision of God in you, and then keeping everlastingly at it, paying the price day by day.

This is what Elbert Hubbard meant when he defined character as the product of two things: first, our mental attitude, and second, the way we spend our time.

Our mental attitude can be our conscious, deliberate effort to keep the purpose of God for our lives ever before us. This is the blueprint of character. And this blueprint becomes engraved on our souls as we worship God daily, exposing ourselves to Him as he is revealed in the life and teachings of Jesus of Nazareth and the great prophets. And the way we spend our time? Isn't this just the matter of day by day, with complete confidence in its rightness, living life in loyalty to that pattern? *Yes, it is costly, but it is worth everything it costs. This kind of living pays dividends daily in happy relationships, meaningful involvement and, ultimately, in eternal life. Jacob was no youngster when he met God. Neither was Paul nor Luther. It is not too late for you or me; that is, if we begin today. We have no promise of tomorrow. We take what we want from life and pay the price—it is all costly. So, take the best.*

El Camino Real

January 31, 1965

Anyone who travels the highways of California eventually finds himself on one called "El Camino Real." If he is intrigued by words and their meanings, he will inquire, hopefully as someone who has an appreciation of history. If he is so fortunate, he will be introduced to such names as Fathers Junipero Serra, Crespi and Gomez. And he will discover that these and a few others first traveled El Camino Real. They did so under directions of the King of Spain, but always and more purposefully under the command of the King of Kings, Jesus the Christ. El Camino Real is "The King's Highway."

These men were missionaries of the Franciscan order. About the time some Boston colonists were dumping a cargo of tea into the bay, Spaniards, working up from Mexico, were claiming what is now California for their country. *They found it populated with Indian tribes eking out a bare existence in a land of sparse rainfall, as yet without irrigation.* True to their vows to serve the poor, and obedient to the command of the King of Kings to "go into all the world and make disciples of all nations," these Franciscan priests were concerned primarily with the native people. So, as they moved up from the South, they established Christian missions, stations in which to preach the gospel, to baptize, and confirm, to marry and finally give Christian burial to the natives. But while they preached to save souls, they did not neglect the bodies of their converts. Each mission was not only a church building but also cultivated fields, herds of cattle and horses, some sheep and goats, chickens and pigs. These, plus orchards and vineyards, made possible by primitive irrigation, brought better health to sick bodies while their spirits were nurtured through the good news of God's love.

From San Diego to San Francisco some eighteen of these stations may be found, following the line, roughly, of present Highway 101. Another interesting fact is that these missions were spaced at intervals to provide a man on horseback with hospitality each night of his journey. And so, a weary traveler found at the end of a day's ride a welcome greeting, a warm bed, good food and companionship, all provided by men who had a sense of mission, a purpose in life growing out of their decision to follow the King of Kings, Jesus Christ.

We have been thinking these past weeks about ways of living. These eighteen missions, marking the trail of those Franciscan priests, are an historic and dramatic answer to our search for a way of life. These are saying to us in visual language, *"Any life worth the living must be a life with a purpose, a sense of mission."* Saying this, they speak to the most urgent need of our life and mind. And the need is particularly urgent because we live in America in the year 1965.

Most of us, I suspect, would agree that today is a great time to be alive. *Measured by the volume of goods we consume, our food, our clothing, our cars, our homes, TV's, airplanes, our bathrooms, and telephones, and even gadgets designed to make our leisure time fun-filled, we have it made.* For what more can the average American ask? Little, except this—*we* have forgotten that we need a worthwhile purpose in living. Jesus knew, "Man does not live by bread alone." An animal may, but not a man. Things, in whatever amount, do not fill some of the needs of the human being. *It is the inner life of man that is sick of starving in America. We try to treat our inner sickness with more things, drugs and alcohol being the current prescription. But they don't heal, and they don't restore health to the soul of man.* What *is* required for this sickness of man's inner life? A sense of purpose and a reason to live.

Notice some of the "good things" in our life which sometimes rob us in subtle ways of this sense of purpose. A man has to work, and every normal man wants to work. But what happens when his work turns out to be a few routine operations on an assembly line, say in a factory? If he has normal powers of physical coordination, he can learn in no time the motions required to turn that screw, to tighten that nut, to spot-weld that particular joint. Or she may be a woman on the belt of a canning operation, sorting the good from the bad prunes. Hour after hour, day after day, the same motions, the same lack of creative and personal demand, a demand which alone can make one's work seem significant to the person.

I am sure every housewife enjoys the emancipation from labor she buys with prepared cake mixes at the supermarket, and we cannot ignore the digestive advantage for those families whose mother never learned to cook. But for mother, the cake is no accomplishment. Anyone who can read simple directions can do as well. And what happens to almost all of us when we move from a small community where we are known and have participated in the community life into a city where no one knows us, and where we have no call to become involved, except perhaps, at election time? *Do you suffer, as I do at times, feelings of total impotence in the face of world issues which are beyond my individual reach? This sense of helplessness can become despair. We may lose all sense of purpose and wonder what life is all about.* Without laboring the point, all of us at times do suffer from this sense of meaninglessness in our daily life. What wouldn't we give for a clear sense of purpose? We are sick in soul without it.

Let me recommend a little paperback for your reading. It is called *Man's Search for Meaning* and was written by the Viennese psychologist Victor Frankl. It is the story of his own imprisonment in a concentration camp during the war and his discovery that only a sense of purpose, a meaningful involvement, saved him and a few others from insanity or suicide. Out of this experience came what is a hopeful approach to mental healing called "Logo-Therapy." Frankl finds that emotional health requires a life of meaningful involvement. He concludes that, not the will to pleasure of Freud, nor the will to power of Adler, but the will to *meaning*, is the basic drive in the human being. The will to meaning lies below and beyond both others.

From the Greek word "*logos*" or "meaning" he draws his title "Logo-Therapy." New to the psychic sciences, it is not new to the religious man. One catches a familiar accent from that concentration camp cell.

We heard it first from a man caught in a totalitarian politico-religious system 2000 years ago... A man who began his public life saying, "I must be about my Father's business," and then, "The Spirit of the Lord is on me, because He has anointed me to proclaim good news to the poor. He has sent me to proclaim freedom for the prisoners and recovery of sight for the blind, to set the oppressed free, to proclaim the year of the Lord's favor."

As He drew near the end of a short but eventful public ministry, He saw a cross looming on the horizon, a death of agony, a symbol of shame, but He could see even in the cross a fulfillment of purpose. *So He said, "And I, if I be lifted up from the earth, will draw all men unto me." Good living and great living are always meaningful living. The Saviorhood of Christ can be spelled out in our time as One who saves us from the hell of meaninglessness by giving us a mission in life.*

Now let us see if we can sketch quickly some meaningful missions to which everyone may devote themselves and, in so doing, find that their journeys take them along the King's Highway, too. Dr. Frankl defines meaning in three categories: "the doing of a deed," "the experience of value in human relationship," and "the creative use of suffering." These three are found supremely in the life of Jesus and in those who follow him faithfully.

Doing a deed... any deed? No, a deed which commends itself because it is worthwhile. I am sure that some of the delinquent behavior of youth and adults is a false attempt to do something that adds meaning to life, even if it is an obnoxious meaning. This seemingly is better than just being ignored completely. But read again the life of Jesus. It is said, "He went about doing *good.*" As you read the gospels you find many of His days were days of doing just what He found to do in response to His sense of mission to mankind. One day He found His friends having trouble with their fishing. He showed them a school of fish on the other side of the boat. When He found an eager spirit, such as Mary, He sat down and talked with her about the deeper things of life. When He met a lonely man whose way of earning money had separated him from his neighbors, He went home with Zacchaeus and talked with him about where life's real values were found. When He found hungry folk, He did what He could to feed them, and it was a lot. When He found a sick man, He healed him. When He attended a wedding and found them short of wine, He helped provide what was lacking. You see, Jesus had a sense of mission, but the fulfilling of it took many forms. He was open and responsive to human need and met it where and when He could.

I saw this way of life advertised in a most unusual place the other day. On one of these roving cement mixers, I read, "We find a need and we fill it." Not bad! *Do you want a meaningful life? Keep your eyes open to the world around you. Find a need and fill it to the best of your ability.* It may be small, but if it is worthwhile to someone else, it is to you.

Then, let us look at the experience of value. Being human, our most fulfilling experiences are those in which another person is involved. We cannot relate totally to an object, a thing, only with a person. And the relationship of love is the only one that is mutually fulfilling for both involved. Love brings out the best in another while it calls for the best in us. Love becomes a doorway to heaven, for each relationship of love represents our highest and most valued experience. So we, as Christians, speak of God as Love. "*God is love; and he that dwelleth in love dwelleth in God, and God in him.*" Jesus gave as his summary of the moral law, "*Thou shalt love the Lord thy God with all thy heart, and with all thy soul, and with all thy mind. And . . . Thou shalt love thy neighbor as thyself.*" Love is the law of great and good living. We, in America, especially, are just now confused about love. We have been sold the idea that sex is love. Sex can be one expression of love, but it can just as easily be the exploitation of another for our selfishness. Love, as honor, respect, concern for another, can exalt the sex relation, making it a sacred and most fulfilling experience. Just as love between parent and child brings out the best in both and love in friendship exalts acquaintance to rich and rewarding experience, so love with sex makes that relationship truly ennobling and fulfilling. Life without love, for someone, a child, a friend, a husband or a wife, is life without meaning.

But one more—we find meaning through suffering. Through suffering? Yes. There is no escape from suffering in this world, some suffering. We try to escape it, but it catches us somewhere. Suffering can destroy us or exalt us. It depends on our attitude and our use of it. Purposeful suffering, as a mother giving birth to a child, is ennobling. Bearing another's burdens lovingly is uplifting, but purposeless suffering destroys us. To paraphrase Nietzsche , he who has a "why" can bear almost any "how." The martyrs had a WHY. The soldier on duty has a WHY. The struggling parent has a WHY, and for all, suffering becomes purposeful and ennobling. Supremely, Christ had a WHY, and the cross became the means for fulfilling that high call to Saviorhood. Won't you join Him, as following His steps you walk *El Camino Real, the King's Highway*, the way of life with a mission? Why not begin *today*?

Thoughts on Collection One

Three messages. Three reasons to take up arms against the world of "things" that distract us from real relationship with each other. Remembering these words were both written and broadcast across parts of our nation nearly sixty years ago, it's curious to me how the ailments all sound so familiar. They could have been written about the things that distract us today. And the consistent prescribed cure is as old as time itself.

I remember thinking after reading these passages, *"When will I wake up?"* and *"What if I actually started to do some of these things?"*

Finding God in Our Daily Contacts helped me revisualize the beauty in the world around me, and again, marvel at it. It served as a springboard of sorts to reconnect me to the Holy Spirit in my daily life; the more I looked, the more I could see and feel it.

It also helped me engage much more purposefully in activities where I could be of some use—civic boards, volunteer projects and, in 2016, an organization my wife and I co-founded called Rock Ranch. That's a story for another time, but part of the wisdom I began gleaning from this message helped me go all in on Rock Ranch. You can see more about it here: www.riderockranch.org

In *Character Is Costly*, I found myself reading and re-reading the bolded statements, only to realize that I kept doing it because, just perhaps, those statements were convicting… me. I had always been pretty dang satisfied with my character and could easily justify times when I let myself take mini-vacations as "situations of circumstance."

What I mean is, at times in the past I would use excuses regularly provided by the world—its accepted behavior, its expectations, its rules, its justice—to justify my personal departures from the character traits I admired most in those I truly respected around me.

It was easy to say, "The world made me do it."

It's like peer pressure, that "everybody's doing it" feeling that gives you permission to excuse bad behavior.

At certain times, in social settings, perhaps when I'd over-served myself beer and booze, I'd invade someone else's conversation, rudely and notoriously loudly, often making fun of someone directly in front of me. My comments and delivery may have been really funny to some people there, but I would immediately realize it troubled me internally. And it certainly hurt the person on the receiving end, even if they laughed it off. Immediately, I needed to find some way to excuse my behavior. Some way the world recognized as palatable. And there are always dozens of worldly excuses from which to draw. Either that, or I woke up guilty the next morning. Needing to make amends. Wishing I hadn't said what I'd said, but able to write it off as "I didn't mean anything by it." And, I would make amends, though embarrassed and frequently frustrated by my actions.

I only wanted to use a circumstance, aided by a little too much to drink, to make the rest of the party laugh at someone else's expense. It's done all the time, and we hope the person on the receiving end can take it. In the event they can't, society tells them to toughen up.

Grandpa's words helped me realize this simply isn't palatable. In fact, it's stupid.

So, for me, that conviction meant I had to find another way to navigate the world. And its occasional social gatherings. Another boat to carry me through rough water back to good, calm waters. A different trail, while rocky and at times steep, that still led me to the summit. A good place. A place where real relationships were more important than popularity. A place where God and I could find each other a little more often, because it certainly wasn't while over-served at some house party.

That's where *El Camino Real* really speaks to me. One of my favorite passages from the chapter includes the following: *Do you want a meaningful life? Keep your eyes open to the world around you. Find a need and fill it to the best of your ability.* This is also something my wife is frequently heard saying inside the hallowed halls of our family. And I've heard Pastor Adam share a similar sentiment on numerous occasions at Embrace Church.

It seems most of my favorite people got there a little sooner than I did. No surprise there, but making a conscience decision to leave the ways of this world in the rearview mirror and focus on those who could use a little help, real help, in the here and now… that's something to think about. That's something *worth* seriously thinking about. And, honestly, a wonderful reason to give "the world" The Heisman.

What about after that? Well, to me, it involves being intentional and a little brave, honestly. Taking a stand for Christ isn't only an internal decision. It's something that eventually becomes a part of who you are in every interaction. And, at times, it means being bolder than you think you can be.

COLLECTION TWO

BE BOLD. WATCH WHAT HAPPENS.

This is an area that gets a little uncomfortable for me. It includes, well, a lot. As I made a decision to leave the ways of "the world" behind, or at least attempted to, I was thrust into a decision. A bold one, as far as I was concerned.

Here's the deal. In order to find out what happens after you've been bold, you actually *have* to be bold. For me, that meant leaving some old ways behind, leaving certain old thoughts behind, even leaving things that were a part of my personality behind. And frankly, I liked the old me.

Ugh. That's uncomfortable.

The next three messages pushed me, and I think they'll push you a little bit, too.

Side note: The date *I Was A Stranger* was first delivered over the airwaves was Valentine's Day, 1965. In this message, Grandpa talks a bit about Martin Luther King Jr. I think it's interesting to note that one month following the delivery of this message, Selma happened. In March 1965. Think about that a bit.

I Was a Stranger

February 14, 1965

"... *I was a stranger, and ye took me in...*" Matthew 25:35 (KJV)

How can you and I know how we are doing as human beings? By what criteria do we judge ourselves? Oh, we have ways of determining our status in various relationships. Our financial success can be measured by Dunn and Bradstreet. We can judge our occupational success by comparison with colleagues and by their judgment of our work. Our doctor will tell us how we are doing physically. Our intelligence is measured by tests and our IQ is recorded. Even our social success is reflected in where we appear in the social register and the number of clubs we join. But none of these, nor perhaps all of them together, tells us how we are doing as a person.

There must be a supreme court to which each of us may carry his case and ask, "How am I doing as a human being, a total human being?" Let me suggest one, perhaps the only one. We will find it described in the twenty-fifth chapter of the Gospel of St. Matthew. Vivid as Eastern literature can be, it still challenges our minds, and our sense of justice, while it captures our imagination. And it goes like this:

When the Son of man shall come in his glory, and all the holy angels with him, then shall he sit upon the throne of his glory: And before him shall be gathered all nations: and he shall separate them one from another, as a shepherd divideth his sheep from the goats: And he shall set the sheep on his right hand, but the goats on the left. Then shall the King say unto them on his right hand, Come, ye blessed of my Father, inherit the kingdom prepared for you from the foundation of the world: For I was an hungred, and ye gave me meat: I was thirsty, and ye gave me drink: I was a stranger, and ye took me in: Naked, and ye clothed me: I was sick, and ye visited me: I was in prison, and ye came unto me.

Well, this *is* different, isn't it? In this word picture, we see the Son of Man, representing all mankind, sitting in judgment. And who is better qualified? But He also represents God, the Creator. For He judges in the light of an internal purpose, the founding of a kingdom "from the foundation of the world." Is this not judgment based upon a *purpose* of man, a purpose indicated in the concept of a Kingdom of God, a God of Love? Is this not another way of saying, "*Man is judged here by his fulfillment or failure to fulfill his possibilities as a human being, a member of the family of man, which is also the family of God?*" I am sure it is. And this, I believe, is a supreme court before which all of us must be judged.

Notice how the writer of this parable of judgment sets up the case to allow no prejudiced testimony and to admit, in support of our case, no hearsay nor philosophical defense but simply the deeds we have done. "In as much as you have done it." And note this as well, we are judged not by our treatment of a friend, a loved one, even a brother, but a *stranger*. He is saying, "You stand highest in the human race when you know how to treat a stranger."

"Am I my brother's keeper?" asked the first murderer. Even a positive answer to this question is not enough. Jesus earlier pointed out that being kind to your neighbor is not enough, if your neighbor is only one whom you know and like. The good Samaritan cared for the perfect stranger, whom he chanced to find on the highway of life. The ancient standard of "loving your neighbor and hating your enemy" will not do, said Christ. To the ancient Jew, a foreigner was an enemy, a stranger, a threat. But in the family of Man, the kingdom of God's concern is extended to the stranger as well as the brother and neighbor. This is a high standard. How do I treat strangers? But in a world where by reason of our growing interdependence, we meet strangers daily, this is not too high a standard. It may be a minimum requirement for living at all. In a time when the outbreak of war would mean the death of some fifty million Americans and an equal number of the enemy in the first few hours, we may experience judgment in horribly realistic terms, a judgment based on this very question, "How do we treat strangers?"

Now this may appear to us as a most unjust arrangement. Does this not mean that the stranger actually sits in judgment upon us? Ought not a man to be judged by his peers? Here in the more marginal matters of our conduct, our peers are competent to judge us by the laws we enact. But we are thinking now of the Supreme Court where God, the Creator, sits in judgment. And in this court the witness whose testimony carried the most weight is not our brother, nor our neighbor, but a stranger. *The question, you remember, is: "How am I doing as a human being?" Not as a Caucasian, not as a Protestant or Catholic, but as a Man.* And it is the stranger who puts our humanity to the severest test. So, in a sense, as with any witness, the stranger becomes our judge.

As Jesus told this parable, could He have been thinking of His own life? He was a stranger to many in Jerusalem. He was a "Stranger of Galilee." Nazareth, a small town of mean reputation. Some asked concerning Him, "Can anything good come out of Nazareth?" He doubtless spoke with a Galilean accent. I don't suppose He dressed like the well-heeled business and professional men of Jerusalem. He wasn't too careful of the customs of the religious community. He wasn't careful of the company He kept, eating with the wrong crowd. He even dared question some of the religious practices and one day made a riot in the very court of the temple because He felt they had turned the house of prayer to a house of profit. The religious leaders of Jerusalem, as well as the secular authorities, didn't like Him. As a stranger with strange ways, He seemed to threaten them. So, what did they do? They killed Him, outside the city wall, where strangers were supposed to die.

But who actually sat in judgment that day? Was it Pilate who allowed Him to be crucified? Was it Caiphas who devised the false procedures of injustice? No, as it turned out, God judged Jerusalem that day. And Jesus, the stranger of Galilee, was the prime witness. Nearly 2000 years of history have not been able to reverse that judgment. *Jerusalem in 33 A.D. was judged by Jesus of Nazareth, a stranger to them because they could not abide His difference in speech, in dress, in custom, in conduct. He was a stranger to them, but no stranger to God, who said of Him, "This is my beloved son."*

But then, as always, God's judgment of man is a prelude to an offer of mercy. By a power which evades our full understanding, this stranger, whose witnesses condemned Him, became for all who would, a Savior to redeem them. "He came unto his own, and his own received him not. But as many as received him, to them gave he power to become the sons of God." And this, I take it, is the way the God of judgment always presides over His world. He closes one door against us, to open a new and better one for us.

May I suggest that these are days of judgment for the human race? And God may be saying to us, "You are judged by your treatment of the stranger. No longer can you indulge yourself in the false security of a closed society. A privileged group. The stranger at your door is your judge and may become your savior. As the father of all mankind, I care equally for all my children. My truth, and my mercy which redeems you, does not always come wearing Western clothes, speaking the English language, through Caucasian lips. I, God, am not a captive of your culture, a servant of your too small concerns."

If our eyes are open to see and our ears open to hear, perhaps we will hear the Christ, God's son, speaking His saving truth in another language other than our own, and see Him walk among us in strange garb, but with the unmistakable purpose of saving the world. I heard it and saw it in a makeshift home, two rooms of what was once a kindergarten attached to a Christian church in Tokyo. *A man and his wife lived there because their home had been bombed during the war. With outstretched hand and open heart, they greeted us who, ten years previously, had been enemies of their country, as they had been of ours.*

The man was nearly blind from disease contracted as he shared the misery of the outcasts of Kobe, Japan. His voice came rasping from vocal cords permanently damaged by tuberculosis contracted the same way. To Toyohiko Kagawa, Christ was not a historic figure only, but a living spirit who called him to live out the love of God for the least of his brethren. This Japanese saint, who died only a few years ago, has laid upon the conscience of the world the sick and hungry and destitute of all nations. He wrote many books, one entitled, *Love and the Law of Life*. For him, the law of love was not a theological abstraction but a command and a power to be translated into human relations. He judges the church today in the name of Christ, while he offers all interpretation of God's will as LOVE spelled in capital letters, working itself out in human well-being.

Sometimes the stranger is in our midst, as Jesus was in Jerusalem, and we reject him. But our rejection is not God's. He is again using what society had rejected to judge and redeem. God, I am convinced, is using the African-American—who, though he lives among us, is a stranger to most of us—using him to judge us, while He offers us a way to larger and fuller life. Finding a voice in Martin Luther King Jr., a disciple of the "King of Kings," God is calling us to judgment and to offer America a new opportunity to become in reality what we like to call "God's Country."

We are being judged by those of African heritage, who have in themselves turned meager opportunity into magnificent achievement, disclosing our racial theories for the myths they are. *They are judging our moral blindness by their sharp discernment of ethical inconsistency in our 300 and more years of economic and social discrimination.* They are judging our condemning complacency in the face of injustice, by their willingness to suffer for a just cause, knowing what we would like to forget, that, "Justice too long delayed is justice denied." They are judging our eager resort to violence with their willingness to suffer rather than return violence for violence.

One sees and hears in these days reminders of some Hebrew youths in a fiery furnace who refused to obey the unjust laws of Nebuchadnezzar, or Paul and Silas singing hymns in a Philippian jail, or the sight of early Christians struggling with the lions in the Roman arena. (Were they the police dogs of Rome?) But even more we hear the words of One crucified as a criminal, but who refused to return evil for evil and could pray, "Father, forgive them, for they know not what they do." *Through this nonviolent protest, we are given an opportunity to repent, to rethink our ways, an opportunity violent revolution would forever deny us.* So it comes round again, this old but ever new day of judgment and opportunity. May God give us the wisdom and the character to see this stranger in our midst as a challenge and opportunity to become true sons of the Father, and inherit the Kingdom brotherhood, inherent in our humanity from the foundation of our world.

The Way of Habits That Help

January 17, 1965

In the fourth chapter of Luke's Gospel, it says of Jesus, that "... as his custom was, he went into the synagogue on the Sabbath day..." If we needed evidence of the humanness of Jesus, this would provide it, for it is the character of the human to act habitually. Taking this clue from the life of Jesus, without question the world's number one citizen, we can afford to give some serious thought to that which we do habitually. We are moved to ask, "Are my habits helping or hindering me?" For I am in reality "a bundle of habits."

William James, psychologist, in his *Talks to Teachers on Psychology*, had this to say about habit. "We speak, it is true, of good habits and of bad habits; but, when people use the word 'habit,' in the majority of cases it is a bad habit which they have in mind... But the fact is that our virtues are habits as much as our vices... Habit is thus a second nature... Ninety-nine hundredths or, possibly, ninety-nine thousandths of our activity is purely automatic and habitual... *The teacher's prime concern should be to ingrain into the pupil that assortment of habits that shall be most useful to him throughout life.* Education is for behavior, and habits are the stuff of which behavior consists. *We must make automatic and habitual, as early as possible, as many useful actions as we can..."*

Good habits are, in a sense, man's Liberator, for they free our attention, enabling us to do several things at one time. Thus, I need not consciously plan each step I take while walking; I can think, talk with a friend, enjoy the scenery and yet walk safely. Only because the various movements in driving become habitual or automatic can we drive a car at all. We could not possibly drive in heavy traffic if most of our actions were not habitually governed. Let your imagination loose on this idea, and you will pray a prayer of thanks to God for giving us the capacity for habitual action. On the other hand, this same capacity for habitual action can make us slaves. How difficult it is to break by conscious attention an act which has become habitual through repetition. Good or bad, our habits are indeed our second natures.

But let's think about some helpful habits—some, perhaps, which we may have overlooked entirely or underestimated at least. Going back to the life of Jesus for a moment, "... as his custom was, he went into the synagogue on the Sabbath day." Note again the wisdom of these ancient giants of our race. The Sabbath itself, recurring every seventh day, was a habit-producing arrangement of the calendar, as though to say, "Unless you keep the Sabbath regularly, it will not become a meaningful part of your life." The practice of worship, as a habit, was enjoined and practiced by the forerunners of our faith, and wisely so. And why make worship an habitual practice? Isn't it a waste of time? Let's think about it a minute.

Worship is by its very nature a discipline of one's attention, one's thoughts, if you will. In worship we deliberately bring into the focus of our mind some great personality, such as Jesus Christ; we may give our serious attention to some aspect of truth which has proven indispensable for good living; we may submit our imaginations to the meaning of some significant symbols; we may be grasped by some sense of responsibility which has hitherto escaped us. "So what?" you may ask. Well, this is what: Do you remember the old saying, "Sow a thought and you reap an act; sow an act and you reap a habit; sow a habit and you reap a character; sow a character and you reap a destiny"? First the thought, then the act, then the habit, and then the character and the destiny. It all begins in the attention but comes out in action.

In Christian worship, the purpose is to bring our attention to focus on the character of God, who we believe to be the personalization of the Highest Good. The late Archbishop William Temple of England once defined worship this way: "In worship we test our knowledge by the wisdom of God; in worship we bathe our souls in the beauty of God; in worship we measure our morals by the holiness of God; in worship we warm our hearts in the love of God; in worship we dedicate our wills to the service of God." When worship becomes a fixed habit in one's life, it becomes one of the determinants in that life.

All of us at times have experiences of worship which are seemingly meaningless. Worship can become a pretty routine business. The occasions when we have been deeply moved by worship, occasions which we remember clearly, are few and far between. But let's liken it to a navigator on an ocean liner. If he consulted his compass when the spirit moved him, when it was convenient, or he happened to think about it, he would be off course most of the time. It's the regular routine correction of the course which finally brings the ship to port. I am sure, if one were lost in a desert for weeks, with no facilities for bathing, the first hot shower would be one never to be forgotten moment. But that every morning routine splash for the day, done habitually, may be no thrill at all. But I ask, "With whom would you rather live—the person who bathes regularly, or the one who just never seems to find the time for it?" Who would you prefer, your neighbor, the person who is guided by the highest personal and social ethics, or the man who never submits himself to the judgment or the inspiration of the highest? We can be sure of this—had Jesus not habitually worshipped, he could not have been the Man of God he was, and thus he could never have been the saviour of men that he is.

I have dealt with this at some length, because we need desperately to face another fact of our life. A recent Gallup poll reveals a steady decline in church attendance by Americans since 1958. And the most marked decline is here on the West Coast. The highest average attendance is in New England, 59 percent; the lowest in the West, 35 percent; the average for the country as a whole being 45 percent. *We have heard much about the moral decline in America. I don't know how this can be measured; but if there is a decline, it can be traced in part to the decline in worship as a habit of life, a habit that really helps to keep us on a high course.*

Consider another habit that truly helps, the habit of reverence in our speech. This may seem to be of minor matter until we recall that our speech is really the mirror of our minds. We draw back the curtain on the privacy of our inner thoughts when we open our mouths to speak. It is true that we never really know a person until we hear him speak to us. The subject of his conversation, the tone of his voice, the choice of vocabulary are all indicators of the real person behind the mask of outer appearance. But speaking not only reveals what we are, it helps create what we will be as well. Who was it who said, "I don't know what I really think until I hear myself say it"? We may smile at that, but this person spoke a profound truth.

The effort required to verbalize our thoughts results in an organization of our thoughts. The act of speaking becomes an act of remembering, too. We never do truly possess an idea until we have expressed it. In giving it away, it becomes ours. Some of us are too self-conscious to express what we think, perhaps for fear of rebuke or ridicule. We may have the courage to compete for a job to earn a living, while we withdraw from the struggle to express ourselves as a means of developing a meaningful life.

Why not make a habit of writing down, in your own words, the meaning of some insight gained, or some meaningful experience? Do it while it is fresh in mind. Every such act will be like adding to your savings account. It will be yours, because you have expressed it. If anything you have heard this morning has begun a train of thought in your own mind, write it down, express it to someone, organize it into some meaning for yourself. Do a bit of it each day. It is as necessary for your intellectual and spiritual growth as three meals a day for your bodily health.

While we are dealing with self-expression, let's say a word about the choice of words. I am always surprised when I hear an educated person using profanity. I make a mental note to the effect that this person is really short on vocabulary. *Profanity, as a habit of speech, is a lazy, careless habit to say the least. The use of the name of God in a profane way adds nothing to the understanding of the subject under discussion.* It isn't even good punctuation. But there is a more serious result of habitually profaning the words of one's religious faith. There is wisdom in the ancient commandment, "Thou shalt not take the name of the LORD thy God in vain..." When this was first given as a guide to habitual speaking, it was given to people who were moving out of one religious culture to another.

The Hebrews were becoming a separate and distinct people. And the distinction was to be in the quality of their personal and social life, a way of life, lived in reverence for obedience to their God, Jehovah. Now what happens when you use irreverently the words which are your authority and your inspiration? Quite obviously, these same words are robbed of their authority and power of inspiration by our careless use of them. *So, for any of us, as well as for the ancient Hebrew, to use the name of God in profanity is to rob it of any meaning for us in prayer.* I can have no faith tomorrow in a God whom I have ridiculed today.

If, when we say the word God, it means only an expletive with which to beat our enemies or regale our friends, that name of God will have no power to guide us, comfort us, challenge us, or inspire us when used in prayer. Profanity is a habit, a destructive habit, in a sense a shameful habit, for it reveals our poverty of speech and our emptiness of ideas.

But consider one other habit that can be most helpful. The practice of living life one day at a time. The converse of that habit is to try living yesterday, today and tomorrow all at the same moment. It is known familiarly as the habit of "worry," and worry is a habit. *Someone called worry the "interest we pay on borrowed trouble."* It is a practice of recalling yesterday's disappointments and problems plus anticipating tomorrow's struggles before they arrive. In either case, there is little one can do about them.

By cluttering today's time with regret from yesterday and fear of tomorrow, we pretty well disqualify ourselves for handling today effectively. Jesus gave us a clue to a better pattern of life. Concerning tomorrow he said, "Take therefore no thought for the morrow... Sufficient unto the day is the evil thereof." Concerning yesterday, Paul counseled, "Let not the sun go down on your wrath, make peace with your neighbor quickly." When we arise in the morning, why not greet the dawn with this affirmation of faith, "This is the day which the Lord has made; we will rejoice and be glad in it."

Each day is a gift from God, given for our use and enjoyment. God has promised, to those who will receive it, sufficient strength and wisdom for each single day. Like the manna of the Old Testament story, it is given enough each day for that day only. When nighttime comes, why not take a few moments to review the day. If there is need for reconciliation with someone wronged, a phone call, a letter to be written, a word of apology to be given, do it then. Having done our best, we can safely leave the rest with God. Someone has suggested this daily cleansing of our spirits is like taking a bath, pulling the plug, and letting the debris go down the drain. Make this a daily habit. Each day can be a joyous adventure, each night a time of restored strength and reborn faith. It's your habits that make you. So may all your habits be helpful in 1965.

The Way of Drift or Decision

January 3, 1965

> The Ways
> *To every man there openeth*
> *A way, and ways, and a way.*
> *And the high soul climbs the high way,*
> *And the low soul gropes the low:*
> *And in between, on the misty flats,*
> *The rest drift to and fro.*
> *But to every man there openeth*
> *A high way and a low,*
> *And every man decideth*
> *The way his soul shall go.*

Thus John Oxenham lays upon our conscience, responsibility for the life we live. This is not to deny the pressure of circumstance, or the limitations of circumstance, but to remind us of what we must never forget, that there is in each of us some capacity to choose, within the limits of our own circumstances, and that capacity becomes our obligation to choose.

We have just discarded our old calendar and opened a new one dated 1965. Many have wished us a happy new year, and I would add mine to theirs. But to those who have lived some years already, the wish may be only a wish. Some will conclude that the only thing new about 1965 will be the calendar. The rest will be a repetition of the old. We may have grown a bit cynical about life, and our only response to the new year's wish is a wish of our own, unsupported by any faith that the future will be better than the past. If you are such, it is to you I wish to speak this morning. Or you may be a young person whose life so far has been devoted to wishing exclusively. If so, I want to speak to you. For I am convinced, that be we young or old, the new year can be new indeed. There is a price to pay, but it is worth it.

Oxenham suggests there are ways of living, but also a way, presumably The Way. He contrasts two, the way of drift or the way of decision. I suggest to you that any hope for a better future for you or for me is to be found not in drift but in decision. Let's see if we can visualize the contrast.

I remember, as a boy, frequent callers at our door, who managed to arrive about mealtime and seemed to know that my parents were incapable of turning a hungry man away. Sometimes they offered to do some small chore in return for a meal. More often they did not. We called them IWWs in the presence of our elders, something else among ourselves. These were depression days, and labor was just beginning to organize. The initials IWW meant "International Workers of the World," an ambitious title for a not-too-ambitious worker, or so we thought. In our adolescent superiority, we translated the letters IWW to mean, "I Won't Work." For whatever sociological, economic or psychological reason, these men were the drifters of our society.

They never seemed to seriously challenge circumstance. They preferred to accept circumstance. They followed the changing seasons to escape the extreme cold, and eked out a sort of existence avoiding the cold shoulders of society in favor of the warmer hearts of the generous and perhaps sentimental among us. They were not bad men, it seemed, seldom in trouble with the law, except a local law against loitering. They made little or no contribution to society, but caused little trouble, either. They were the economic drifters. I suspect when they finally found the rigors of the road too much, they would settle in a city mission somewhere, become "soup bowl saints," and, when death came, be laid in a pauper's grave. The world is little better for their having lived and probably not much worse.

Most of us don't belong to the economic drifters, but what of other relations to society? Do we challenge other circumstances of our living, or are we inclined to take the path of least resistance? I am thinking now of our temptation to conform to social practices which we find a bore and waste of time and energy. Do others make decisions for us simply because we are too unconcerned to make our own? I listened recently to a physician who works largely with those struggling with alcohol addiction. He pointed out that most of us become addicted as we yield to social pressure, doing what is expected of us rather than what our own judgment or desire would indicate for us. Ours has been called the "age of conformity," a time when we lose our identity as persons in our willingness to be absorbed in the mass of our social set. *We follow the seasons socially. We are drifters socially.*

One of the tragic effects of this tendency to drift through life is seen in our growing divorce rate. No one who has tried to build a stable and secure home life will say it is easy. Those who have will also agree that it is one of life's greatest achievements. But it is an achievement. I am not suggesting that there are no situations in which separation is not necessary for the well-being of all concerned. *I am saying, however, that to surrender to circumstances is to take the easy way, or so it may seem, the easy way out.* We may try to defend our practice of what someone has called "tandem polygamy" by calling it "freedom" when in all honesty we ought to call it "failure." To drift from one love nest to another is not strength but weakness, getting an emotional handout here, another there. Successful marriage requires work and wisdom, self-control and self-expression, love and loyalty, faith and fidelity. These are achievements, not accidents. Without them the love drifter eventually is reduced to emotional pauperism.

But I am thinking too of religious drifters. Judged in terms of church affiliation, America is a religious nation. Something over 60 percent of our people throughout the nation belong to some religious fellowship. That is true except in California. I cannot document these figures but was told recently that, in the Bay Area of California, only 17 percent of the people are actively related to any church or religious group. In other parts of the West Coast, it runs to about 24 percent. What does this say about us? Many of us have come from other parts of the country where we were involved in the life of our religious fellowship. Did we become tired of the responsibility? *Are we indulging the freedom from responsible living which anonymity brings, as we live in larger cities? Have we become religious panhandlers, taking enough to get by from those who are generous enough to share, but never contributing anything significant through responsible involvement ourselves?*

And what of our political drifting? I was pleased to read recently that over 70 million Americans voted in the last election, the highest ever. That is all to the good. But are we interested enough to become informed politically? Do we trouble to study and discuss the issues before us as free citizens?

We who live in Berkeley, especially, and all Californians may have been disturbed, perhaps shocked, by the demonstrations on the campus of the university. Though the issues may not be clear to all, and though we may abhor disorder, this much we can approve, namely, the willingness of young men and women who, believing they have a just cause, are ready to pay the price of involvement in winning a cause.

Day after tomorrow, some 800 students will stand trial for standing up to be counted. It is a gratifying discovery to find folks who will not conform to what they are convinced is injustice. *They may be too impatient, but when does patience become capitulation? They may talk too much, but when does silence become surrender?* Out of this struggle will come a stronger and finer university, and out of this university will come leaders who have learned that costly decision is the price one must always pay for progress in personal and social life. America and the world need this kind of leadership.

But how does one move from the drift to the decision as a pattern of living? We shall have to believe that LIFE spelled in capital letters is always the disciplined life. We of the Christian faith have been exposed all our lives to the inspiration of One who not only taught but demonstrated that "The meek (disciplined) inherit the earth" and that "straight is the gate and narrow the way that leads to life… while broad is the way that leads to destruction." If we have any doubt about that, we will never have the firmness of purpose to make those costly decisions.

But look about you. No man has achieved greatness in science who has not said "yes" to the discipline of science, and "no" to the enticements which would divert his attention and steal his time. No musician has ever performed to his own satisfaction or the enjoyment of others who has not narrowed down his concerns, to give himself with devotion to a choice of interest. No man has achieved a leadership with its control of others without first learning the hard lessons of self-control. No man has achieved excellence of character, the kind of personal stature to which others can look for inspiration, without saying a decisive "no" to some things and an equally decisive "yes" to others.

A leader of men is never a drifter. People need no leadership in drifting, that just comes naturally.

Let me indicate some practical steps, which, if followed, will make our living more productive, and thus happier because we have abandoned drift for decision.

First, think through to a clear image of the person you want to be, the goal you want to reach. Maybe it is improvement in your work. Maybe it is a better home life. Maybe it is a more meaningful participation in the community. But let's be specific about it. Vagueness at this point is sure defeat. Then it is a good thing to share these decisions with someone who can help us think clearly about them and what is equally important, and by their knowing, help us to hold to our course. We don't like to fail in the eyes of others, you see.

Then, keep that image clear by regular reference to it. Review the objective. We in the church worship regularly for this very reason, to keep the goal of life clearly in view. The Christian accepts Christ as his goal but recognizes the need to check his direction and progress regularly. It isn't always a comfortable exposure. In Shakespeare's *Othello*, Iago says of Cassio, "He hath a daily beauty in his life that makes me ugly." But the person of Christ inspires, while His beauty judges us. So, we will regularly review our goals in life. The purpose will inspire, while it judges our failure. This is opportunity for correction. And let us never forget that greater effort and more energy is no solution, if we are moving in the wrong direction.

Finally, define the immediate steps, which, if followed, will bring us eventually to that desired goal. Any worthwhile objective is not achieved in a single effort. It is usually a series of efforts. So, the decision will focus daily on the steps, knowing that each step brings us closer to the goal. *If it is better character, then the daily devotion and the daily response to both the judgment and inspiration of worship is required.* If it is work improvement, the decision must be to improve today's work, and today's work will contribute to tomorrow's improvement. If it is a better home life, we decide daily on those small items and acts, which add up to the home life we want. And may I reiterate, effective decision is always a combination of the will and the imagination. So, keep the imagination alive and clear with frequent return to the dream. And decisions are daily decisions... "Choose you this day whom you will serve."

Yes, it will be a happier new year as we move from drift to decision.

Thoughts on Collection Two

When I finished with those three messages, I was like, "Thanks a lot, Grandpa." Sarcasm intended.

But I also dreamed of someday having the kind of courage it takes to be that bold. To make decisions about how I would conduct myself at home, at work, with my kids, my friends, and yes, total strangers.

Some of the things I thought about, and still think about today, are ways I can better learn how to discern the mind of Christ in my daily activities and interactions. I am *so far* from perfect. Good gravy, I am 100 miles from even adequate sometimes.

But I'm trying. Every day. Lord willing.

I want to be open to others, help the stranger, live with character and a conviction to worship the One who gave me life. In great abundance. I cannot waste it. I can't look myself in the mirror any longer and be... satisfied. It's boring. It's dull and it won't help this world, at all.

In short, in my daily prayers I am asking for help to "chase the favor of God." That's not my line. That one belongs to a man named Sam Collier. He gets after the concept pretty well in a book called, *A Greater Story*.

So, what have I done, practically speaking?

I am teaching myself to have difficult conversations, to get comfortable being uncomfortable.

I am seeking out an expanded network of people who do not do what I do. The kind who don't hang out with people who do what I do. I want to learn how to have real relationships with people who may be different from me. I do this by reaching out, with intention, to people I do not know but would like to.

The people I find interesting. Even disagreeable at times. I want to understand if it's possible to develop some kind of relational civil discourse, born from Christ's love for the stranger, in an effort to understand people a little bit better. This is the lesson I am learning from *I Was a Stranger*.

So, how am I doing with it? Well, let's just say that the staff of Josiah's Coffee House in Sioux Falls, South Dakota is getting to know me pretty well. It is a rare week when I am not meeting someone there for a cup (black, no froufrou) at least two and sometimes even three mornings a week. In short, it's been awesome. Truly. I recommend stretching the boundaries of familiar relationships to anyone without reservation. It'll be uncomfortable at times. But I'm getting comfortable with being bold, and God is blessing these conversations and helping guide me into new friendships.

I'd be remiss if I didn't also say this…

I'm not always proud of the way in which I think about people. I love the way my grandfather looks at people through his words in these chapters. I have to remember that he wrote these messages in his mid to late fifties. He'd already been pastoring people for over thirty years. He knew them. He'd developed an understanding of human behavior as perhaps only a pastor can.

Even though I've had thirty plus years of experience with people, I can still see them very easily as products of their choices, not always immediately as children of God. It's natural, I suppose. But I am growing less fond of my instant reactions to people who are "drug addicts," "cheaters," "liars," "losers," "gay," "lazy" and the list goes on.

Through the words of my grandfather from over fifty years ago, I am praying I can begin to more quickly see each of these people as children of God… first. It's hard for me. Maybe it's hard for you, too. But, in the moments I am able to do it, my level of frustration and instant dismissal subsides. When I catch the faintest glimpses of the love Jesus has for everyone, when I catch a whisper of His love in my mind first… well, I believe every thought, word, conversation and relationship is so much better. Calmer. Human.

I am able to avoid *The Way of Drift or Decision* by keeping close connection to the *The Way of Habits that Help.*

My family and I are really excited about our church home. We have been attending a newer church regularly since about 2017. We started attending because our daughter became a part of their very organized and talented worship team. She now helps lead worship nearly every Sunday she's home from college. Hers is another story, for another time. But her involvement is how we initially became involved.

Prior to this church, we had been longtime members of another. We were married in our former church, baptized the kids in the former church, found Christ while attending that former church, and we love the membership and people who still attend that former church.

We just had to make a change for ourselves. And we've done so.

I used to get excited for weekends because they meant a night (or two) out on the town, in the pub or getting into some other kind of mischief with friends. And, to be honest, we still fill our weekends with stuff like that from time to time. But the reason I look forward to the weekends now really has more to do with Sundays than anything else.

I can't believe I am more excited to go to church during the weekend than I am to do just about anything else. If you want to see the Lord working in your life, I recommend finding the church that causes that response in you and your family. Seriously. It is incredible.

I made the decision to make church a priority much earlier in my life, and now we're attending a church that is turning my priority into passion. Passion for Christ and His will for our world. That's crazy. But it's happening. And I have the messages found in "*Be Bold*" to thank for it.

Last note, along the "*Watch What Happens*" line of thinking.

I am amazed at who else has become demonstrably interested in the church. Both of our sons and one significant other are also attending regularly with us! There are many other stories about the boys here, and those, too, will have to wait. But three kids in their late teens and early twenties

Collection Two: Thoughts on Collection Two

going to church with their parents on a very regular basis. In today's world?! That's not something we expected. So, now we're all in the mix.

Nearly every week.

Together. I love it. Just love it.

Praise God.

What follows in Collection 3 are messages related to being intentional about choosing love as our first means of interaction with the people of our world. Making an effort. Making the choice. Not sitting on the fence. It does require leaving some of the ideas and thoughts of "the world" in the rearview, and it forces us to be bolder than we'd like to be at times.

But it works. Read on.

COLLECTION THREE

Intentional Love in All Relationships

What does this truly look like?

How do you decide who you're going to choose to love intentionally?

Am I *choosing* to love through sincere interest? Out of loyalty? Out of mutual respect?

What does this really look like?

My grandfather was really onto something when he delivered the next few messages. I was completely blown away. Again, the wisdom of these sermons came from the heart and mind of a Dakotas-raised soul who found himself in Berkeley, California during the final ten years of his ministry!

From the Dakotas of the 1920s, '30s, '40s and '50s to the California of the 1960s.

Wow. Think about that. Who knows? Maybe it could be time for something like that to happen again!

Side Note:

I'm actually writing these words overlooking the beautiful, majestic cliffs in Little River, Northern California. Watching the waves crash playfully, and sometimes violently, into the rocky shoreline. It's something to see.

We came to California to attend another event and to spend some time together, as COVID had robbed us of our twenty-fifth wedding anniversary trip!

Prior to arriving here, however, my wife and I made a quick stop in Berkeley at the last church my grandfather parished before his retirement. The church is called Epworth, and it's still a Methodist church in a really nice neighborhood. Historic and well maintained. I know another particular pastor who likes neighborhoods like this one. He lives a little closer to home in Sioux Falls.

Anyway, we were fortunate to find the church open on a Friday afternoon, and inside were several people going about the business of the day. I introduced myself to the first person I met and explained who I was and why I was stopping by.

Overhearing the conversation was a silver-haired woman who seemed friendly enough when she asked, "What was your grandfather's name?"

"C. Maxwell Brown," I replied.

"I knew your grandpa," she said. "He's the reason I joined this church!"

Wait. What?! My grandfather ministered at Epworth from 1963 until 1967.

"I joined in 1966," she said.

That was fifty-six years ago. Surreal to say the least.

The woman's name is Barbara, and she proceeded to give us one of the greatest walks down memory lane I've had in a long while. We toured the sanctuary, the library and some of the newer places the church had expanded into as well. In all, we spent about forty-five minutes with her, and I could easily see that Grandpa Max had made an impression all those years ago. She remembered him very fondly and still could recall several of his sermons. I loved it. That was really, really cool.

My grandpa had made that kind of impression in 1966. That was his thirty-eighth year of ministry. In that time, he had poured out the love of Christ into congregations all over the Dakotas and now was doing it in California. In order for that kind of love to take, it must have come from somewhere else. Somewhere beyond Grandpa.

I think that's what the love of Christ does for people when applied liberally, not forcefully. It has a universal appeal, an attractiveness. It was attractive to a young woman (at the time) like Barbara and so many thousands of others over Grandpa's ministerial call. It's something we should be continuously striving for in our daily relationships as well. And it looks something like what follows.

Childhood's Bill of Rights

January 1964

Since human life means constant change, from birth through childhood, youth, maturity and old age, any religion worth the name must be a faith for *all* of life. It must have something to support the child, to challenge the youth, to fortify the mature adult and to enrich and sustain the life of old age. This our Christian faith does. And today we turn our attention to childhood. And since children are the most dependent group in the human family, we will consider Christianity's contribution to childhood under the title "A Child's Bill of Rights." These rights are not something the child can demand and possess on its own. They are rights which grow out of the needs and nature of every child, rights required by God in providing for the life, growth and maturing of His creation. I have the conviction that if the basic rights of childhood can be achieved, we will be well on the way to a truly civilized life, in fact on the threshold of the Kingdom of God.

It was this fact, I suspect, which moved Christ to give childhood its high place in the scale of human importance. When asked who was the greatest among men, he took a child and placed him beside him and said, "... for he that is least among you all, the same shall be great." And in another instance he said, that if anyone should cause a little child to stumble, it would be better for that man that a millstone should be tied about his neck and he be dropped into the deepest sea. Strong language? Yes, but also strong conviction growing out of deep insight. What, then, are some of the rights of childhood, provided in any Christian community?

In the first place, it is a child's right to be born into a family. It is his right, because the family is the native habitat of the child. It is to a child what environment is to any growing thing. It nourishes and supports his life. We Christians believe this is ordained of God and indicated in the needs of the child himself.

Christianity began in a family, when a babe named Jesus was born into the home of Mary and Joseph. It is the Christian conviction that Jesus would not have been who and what He was had He not lived in a home, known the guidance of parents and the discipline of life involving other individuals. From infancy to manhood, He lived in a home. *We can never consent to the notion that there is an equally good substitute. We can never endorse the idea of children born and nurtured apart from their parents as a desirable thing.* Whether it be in state-sponsored programs such as were practiced in Nazi Germany for a time, and also in Communist Russia for a time, nor resulting from the indifferent attitude of many Americans who seem to consider children, their own especially, a trial and nuisance.

It is the Christian's conviction that marriage is a sacred institution and includes in its purposes the providing of a home for children. Psychologists support this stand, after dealing with the heartbreaking cases of children who have been denied the normal environment of a home. Believing in Childhood's right to be born into a home, we can reach no other conclusion than that no adult has a right to bring a child into the world without providing at home.

And this leads inevitably to that second basic human right for every child, the right to love and be loved. For only in the relationship of love can he come to know himself as someone with a sense of his own worth. This sense of worth comes from that somebody who lets us know our worth, through His love of us. A child without love becomes a warped, twisted, and spiritually deformed person, a burden to himself and a threat to those around him. The records of children in trouble with society leave no doubt that the child who is in conflict with the world about him is striking back at a world that is against him, a world that is a jungle, every man for himself, in short, a world without love.

So basic is love to the life of a child that God in His wisdom has made it nigh impossible for a mother to give birth to a child without a most imperative need on her part to give the child her affection. The Christian faith is rooted in the conviction that God is love, that the nature of our being, our very existence, depends on love. So, it's no accident that where Christian faith has been taught and practiced, human life beginning with the life of a child has become a sacred thing.

Yes, the childhood Bill of Rights includes the right to love and to be loved. As adults, we have no more justification for denying love to a child than we have for denying it food or drink.

But consider another inalienable right of every child. Every child has a right to be understood by his elders. How often have you spoken harshly to your child and closed with, "Now I want you to UNDERSTAND me," and if he is a young child, he probably understands nothing except that for some reason this big person is making a lot of threatening noises. But have you ever said to yourself, "Now I want to understand that boy or that girl"? Do we understand, for instance, that a child born into an adult world, where everything is arranged for the convenience of adults, is in a pretty formidable and confusing world?

Have you ever tried to get around in a country where you had no knowledge of the language? Well, every child goes through that frustrating experience. What if you were suddenly precipitated into a world where everything is twice as large as it is now? What if you had to stand on tiptoe to open every door? What if the chairs were so high your feet never touched the floor? What if knives and forks at the table were twice as big and twice as heavy as they now are, and the glass so big around that you couldn't hold it in one hand and were embarrassed to grasp it with both. What if you couldn't see out of a window without climbing on a chair or sofa? You see, it's a big world for little ones, with all the problems such a mismatching brings. Do we stop to understand that about a child?

Collection Three: Childhood's Bill of Rights

One father I heard about made that discovery, albeit and a bit tardily, and wrote what he titled, "The Shrine of Sleeping Childhood." It's written by a penitent father, who slipped into his son's bedroom at night, finding him fast asleep, a hand crumpled under a cheek, curly hair damp on his forehead, and out of some remembrances of the day wrote the following words.

> I scolded you when you were dressing for school because you just gave your face a dab of water and wiped it on the towel. Then at breakfast you put your elbows on the table. You spilled things, you gulped your food, and spread the butter on your bread too thick. When you started off to school you called back, "Goodbye, Dad," and I just shouted, "Hold your shoulders back." Then when I came home from work I found you on your knees playing marbles. And you had holes in your trouser knees. And I reminded you that trousers cost money. Humiliating you before your friends, I marched you home to change your clothes. Then in the evening while I was reading the paper you came quietly into the room, timidly with a sort of hurt look in your eye, and I said, "What do you want now?" And you didn't say a word, but with one tempestuous lunge you were in my lap, your arms around my neck and kissing me goodnight. And then you slipped down and I heard you pattering up to bed having expressed a love that not even my coldness and neglect could destroy. It was then that I began to see what was happening. And this is what has happened.
> It is not that I do not love you. It is that I expect too much of you. I was measuring you by the yardstick of my own years. I have asked much, too much. Hereafter I will repeat as a ritual, "He is nothing but a boy, a very little boy." I have come back tonight to ask for forgiveness, for being so stupid as to not to understand that simple thing.

Yes, a child has a right to be understood as a little person trying to get along in a big world.

Who has not wished to know what was in the mind of a child? Somewhere I picked up this list of "don'ts for parents," as compiled from children who were encouraged to express what they thought.

Don't be a dictator. They make us angry, afraid and dumb.

Never hit us. We might get the idea that it's alright for big nations to rule little nations by hitting them.

Don't embarrass us by finding fault with us before our friends or yours.

Don't treat us like cute pets, or dressed up dolls, or puppets. We are people.

Don't laugh *at* us ever. Laugh *with* us often.

Don't be afraid to let us make mistakes. How else will we or you know that our way isn't better than yours?

Don't be afraid to talk to us. We see through you easily. But we are quite tolerant of growing up. Don't talk down to us.

Don't be unjust. Take some time to judge. Use sparingly the powers you have, but we lack. Often you drive us to deceit and meanness to get even. Let's have no struggle for power among friends.

YES, A CHILD HAS A RIGHT TO BE UNDERSTOOD, as a little person trying to get along in a big world.

Finally, every child has a right to a faith by which to live. To rationalize our spiritual laziness by deciding, "I want my child to choose his own faith when he is grown up" is as indefensible as to say, "I won't get my child an education. I will let him choose what he wants to know when he is grown up." *A child can't wait until he is grown to have a faith. He must know what to believe about himself, to understand the meaning of love and hate, to have an idea of what constitutes the good life.* He needs some key to interpret the mysteries of life, of which he is likely to be more aware than we adults are. He needs to know the meaning of tragedy, for young lives do experience tragedy. He needs to know what to do with his guilt feelings, for he has them in abundance. He needs to know something about death, for he encounters it long before he is an adult. *He needs what every person needs, some way to relate to the reality of life we call God, since we know no better name for Him.* And we who are Christians are convinced that all these needs are met most fully in the life of Jesus of Nazareth, and that He who took little children to cuddle them is the supreme personal example for a child to admire and emulate.

And when I say we, I mean we who are parents. For parents are the first teachers of children. We learn from example before we learn from words. Ray Stannard Baker put it complete when he said, speaking of his father, *"When I thought how much my father admired God, I had a high opinion of Him."* Your child has a right to faith, and if he is to have one, it is likely he will receive it from you.

The rights of man! How we cherish and protect them. But the rights of a child? Are we ready to guarantee him a home in which to live, a love that is the native habitat of a growing life, understanding that makes growth an orderly and progressive achievement, and, finally, a faith to guide his choices and inspire his hopes? These are his right. Only we as adults can guarantee them for him. He cannot possess them himself as a child.

For the Loneliness that Desolates Us

September 15, 1963

And the LORD God said, "It is not good that man should be alone..."
Genesis 2:18 (KJV)

"Behold, the hour cometh, yea, is now come, that ye shall be scattered, every man to his own, and shall leave me alone: and yet I am not alone, because the Father is with me." John 16:32 (KJV)

"... lo, I am with you always, even unto the end of the world."
Matthew 28:20 (ASV)

Several years ago, a popular song climbed rapidly to the top of the hit parade. The title of that song was this, "You'll Never Walk Alone." As I remember it, the title was its greatest asset, but its popularity sky-rocketed nonetheless, for it assured people that at no time and under no circumstances would they ever be totally abandoned, they would never have to be alone. As I say, it was a hit.

And it was a hit tune because, of all the experiences of mankind, there is nothing he dreads more than loneliness, unless it is death, and to man death means separation, fears, loneliness. So, when the Bible writer in Genesis told the story of creation, he had God say, "It is not good that man should be alone." Now, though we might be constrained to debate some issues with God, on this we find ourselves in complete and enthusiastic agreement. So sure are we that loneliness is to be avoided, as one would avoid death itself, that we have judged "solitary confinement" as second only to the death sentence as punishment. If this is true, and I am sure it is, then I am also sure that our faith must have something to offer its people when they stand face to face with the spectre or the reality of loneliness.

And our faith does just that. The whole creation story turns out to be a story of God dealing with the problem of loneliness, His own first of all, making Man in His image and keeping company with him in the Garden of Eden. Man's loneliness, unfilled by all other animals of the world, was met only when God gave woman to man for his companionship. And the tragic element of the scriptures is built out of those experiences of man which separate him from God and from his fellow man. Loneliness then, is a major concern of God, as it is a major problem of man. So, it may just be that our problem and God's concern brought together may issue in a saving solution. Indeed, that is the promise of Christ… "… lo, I am with you always, even unto the end of the world."

Loneliness is a universal malady, a sickness of the soul of the human race. But its universal character in no degree assuages the pangs of my individual agony. If misery loves company, as we are told, the misery of loneliness should love it the more. But we discover that our need for companionship lies too deep for treatment with platitudes or even social organization. It is to our credit that in our day we are beginning to see more deeply into the human soul, and to find that man is more than a gregarious animal whose loneliness is cured by membership in the herd. No, we are discovering that there is nothing so lonely as a crowd, and sociologist David Reissman could write a popular book by the title *The Lonely Crowd*. You and I know from experience how true this is. Tokyo, Japan, is the largest city in the world. Yet I was never lonelier than walking down the Ginza. There was hardly room to walk, but, though jostled in the throng, I was desolate in spirit. The barrier of language shut me out of their lives and shut them out of mind. One can ride a packed bus or a full plane, and, while imprisoned with dozens of people for hours at a time, our loneliness is not thereby cured.

There are homes made bleak with loneliness. Husband and wife may sit across the table from each other seven days a week and remain in a state of unrelieved loneliness. There are children in homes with parents eating at the same table, sleeping under the same roof, sharing the same economic security, but so far removed in spirit as to not know each other. They speak, but do not communicate anything of themselves. Misunderstanding has lowered, not an iron curtain, but a curtain of mistrust between parent and child, and both may be desolate in their isolation of spirit. Some of us live in apartments. We hear footsteps above us and beside us. But those steps give us little sense of community, for though we may know the name of our neighbor, we know little else and are not inclined to find out more. This is the loneliness which seems a universal plague on all of us.

Then there are circumstances of life which deepen our sense of isolation. Consider illness. A two-hundred-bed hospital is almost inevitably a two-hundred-cell prison, where physically ill people are suffering "solitary confinement," for acute illness is a solitary business. Oh yes, doctors and nurses can ease the pain and friends bring in flowers to distract attention from our loneliness for a moment. But this thing which threatens a person is his alone, and it is something no one can share. The moment of illness occupies his whole world. And it's a lonely world.

I shall never forget a teenaged girl who was critically ill. I stepped into her room to find her under the oxygen tent, another symbol of our separation from the outer world, even though it is bringing us a chance for physical life. I visited quietly for a moment, and then I observed her trying to wriggle her hands under the edge of the tent. When she succeeded, she grasped my hand, just to feel the touch of another person and thus dispel some of the loneliness. Sickness can be a lonely vigil with people all around, for *it shuts us in as it shuts others out.*

Is there any significance in the fact that *The Lonely Crowd* was written by an American about Americans? I don't know, really, but I believe that our emphasis on "individualism" does have some unpleasant side effects. Our cult of achievement, to outstrip everyone else, does provide incentive for personal effort. America loves a winner, whether it be in sports or in a business or in politics. But there is loneliness in individual achievement. Who was it that said the throne is the loneliest seat in the world? The lonely heights of personal achievement are not imaginary places but real experiences.

The successful is never quite sure that people seek him out because they like him personally or because they wish to bask in the brightness of his limelight. The man of wealth is often a lonely man for the same reason. He may have people about him constantly, but he may ask, "Are they interested in me for what I am or what I have?" And if the answer is the latter, then he knows the burden of loneliness. I suppose most of us would be willing to suffer a bit of loneliness at the cost of being rich or famous, but it is real, nevertheless.

Then there is the desolation that follows the death of a loved one. Some seem never to recover from it. George Santayana spoke for all the bereaved when he wrote:

> With you a part of me hath passed away;
> For in the peopled forest of my mind
> A tree made leafless by this wintry wind
> Shall never don again its green array.
> Chapel and fireside, country road and bay,
> Have something of their friendliness resigned;
> Another, if I would, I could not find,
> And I am grown much older in a day.
> But yet I treasure in my memory
> Your gift of charity, and young hearts ease,
> And the dear honour of your amity;
> For these once mine, my life is rich with these.
> And I scarce know which part may greater be,
> What I keep of you, or you rob from me.[3]

Yes, the loneliness which follows the death of a loved one is desolate, indeed.

Then there is what someone has defined as our "cosmic loneliness," our feeling of lostness in the vast measureless reaches of this ever-expanding physical universe. Is there another who knows me as a person and, knowing, cares? Was the confidence of Christ, that when all His disciples deserted Him, He would still not be left alone, was this just a delusion?

Ah, our Christian faith says no, this is not delirium, but the discovery of all man's findings. And it is the discovery which gives us that sense of being at home in our universe, among the immensities of space or in the confinements of a prison cell. *For this faith breaks through the prison walls of our self to set us free, to love other persons and be loved in return.* And it is this discovery which so fills our inner emptiness that space itself is no spiritual vacuum, but rather the dwelling place of the Most High. Let's see how it comes about.

Most of us suffer from "self-consciousness." Sometimes this self-consciousness makes us timid and afraid of people. Sometimes it makes us obsessed with our own concerns. Whether we are too timid or too preoccupied with ourselves, our self-consciousness shuts us out of other people's lives, and shuts others out of our lives. Our timidity says to other people, "Don't approach me, I don't want anything to do with you." And we are passed by, because others will not invade our self-chosen seclusion.

Our preoccupation—self-consciousness again—seems to others: "You are not important to me. Don't bother me." And so others avoid us, wanting to be spared the hurt of a rebuff. So, we are alone. And in our relation to God, self-consciousness shuts us in our prison and out of His presence. *Faith is our daring response to God's relationship of trust, and fellowship with God.* Our preoccupation with ourselves leaves no room nor time for God, and so He remains only a word, a vague unreality.

Whether it be between friends, between lovers, between a man and his God, the barrier is our self-concern. *Our faith insists that in all relationships concern for the other person is basic. This is the true meaning of love.* Our love for our mate, our child, our friend and our love for God dissolves the barriers which shut us out of true fellowship. So, the command "Thou shalt love" comes back again. There is no substitute, no way around. But why should we fight it? It is Christ's answer to our fatal illness, the sickness of our souls, and we live in isolation from one another and from God. To all the lonely in the world the invitation is "Come, and learn through love," and your loneliness is filled for today and for all of your tomorrows.

For the Joys that Invite Us

September 29, 1963

"These things have I spoken unto you, that my joy might remain in you, and that your joy might be full." John 15:11 (KJV)

"If ye know these things, happy are ye if ye do them." John 13:17 (KJV)

The "pursuit of happiness" is one of the unalienable rights guaranteed American citizens in our constitution. There of course is no guarantee that we find it. But long before there was an American nation, or an American constitution, the pursuit of happiness was engaging the time and attention of mankind. For the quest of happiness and joy is a universal quest.

This search for happiness takes many forms. The young man, whose fancy in spring turns to thoughts of love, hopes to find happiness in turning those thoughts into experience. The businessman piling up stocks and bonds, neglecting his family and his community, does what he does because he assumes, mistakenly perhaps, that this road leads to joy and happiness. Even the housewife scrubbing the floor, goes through the drudgery of housekeeping because she is happier when the house is clean than when it is not. I suspect even the martyr is a martyr because he is happier obeying the command of his conscience than he would be living a life of self-condemnation should he betray his highest ideals.

So must it have been with Latimer and Ridley[4], whose deaths are memorialized by a stone cross on Oxford Street. For, the story goes, that as they were being hauled to the fire for burning, Hugh Latimer called across to Ridley, "Be of good comfort, Master Ridley, and play the man. We shall this day light such a candle by God's grace in England as I trust shall never be put out." And it hasn't.

We will soon be celebrating the Last Supper on World Communion Sunday. You remember when Jesus met with His disciples for the last time before His arrest and crucifixion, knowing He was to die, He broke bread to symbolize His broken body and poured out wine to symbolize His blood being drained from His body. The story relates that when the meal was complete, they sang a hymn and then left the room to go out to Gethsemane. And what was the hymn they sang? A hymn of praise to God, a hymn of triumphant joy. The writer to the Hebrews speaking of Jesus had this to say, "… who for the joy that was set before him endured the cross, despising the shame…" What kind of person is this, and what kind of faith is this that inspires men to sing on the threshold of death?

This leads us to ask the question, "Does Christianity give us a faith which, when adopted and practiced, leaves its devotees a deposit of inner peace and joy?" I insist that if we have the genuine article, then our investment in that faith will pay dividends in abiding joy and inner happiness.

Some have insisted that the pursuit of happiness does not lead us to Christianity.

I suspect "heresy," a term given to aberrations of religion which depart from the true faith, has been most destructive to our faith. It has not been anything doctrinal at all but a sad caricature of Christianity which goes under the name of the genuine article. The emphasis on "Jesus, the man of sorrows" is understandable but not defensible. Let us not forget the common people heard Him gladly. Let us not forget that little children loved Him, and the little child is instinctively drawn to one whose face is lit with kindliness and joy, while he shrinks from a sad and melancholy person. Jesus had much to say about the joy of living. "Rejoice and be exceedingly glad,"

He said, and what is more, He pointed clearly the direction we must travel if our pursuit of happiness is not to end in disillusionment and despair.

Jesus holds before us the appeal of happiness and joy, rather than pleasure, and I suspect our failure to find happiness stems from our failure to distinguish between the two. Pleasure may indeed lead to joy and happiness, but often it does not. They are related but not identical. *We are insatiable pleasure seekers but, judging by the growth of mental illness among us, we have not found happiness in that search.* And here is why.

We have tried to settle for pleasure rather than happiness.

I remember back in 1944, while driving my car one day to an outlying prairie church, I heard Bishop Fulton J. Sheen preaching over the radio. He was talking about the difference between pleasure and happiness and the relationship of the two. I have always remembered one distinction he made. *Pleasure is an experience of the senses, something we see, hear, taste or feel. Happiness is of the mind and can be quite independent of the senses.*

He went on to point out that not pleasure but happiness must be the goal of life, because pleasure operates on the law of diminishing returns, while happiness does not. Too much pleasure can turn to pain. You may like filet mignon, but if you had to eat it three times a day forever, you'd come to hate it. A beautiful flower is a delight to the eye but seen exclusively would soon tire us. A symphony may delight the ear, but if one was forced to hear it incessantly forever, he would come to hate it. For the same reason sexual overindulgence can become anything but pleasurable. And all because man is more than an animal, whose life must be fulfilled by more than sense experience. Pleasure that does not satisfy the mind as well as the body is a snare and a delusion. And here our basic nature as eternity-oriented is illustrated. Joys of the mind are not subject to circumstance. They have to do with the inner life and thus are not dependent on circumstance, which is constantly changing.

Christ, however, does not discount pleasure. He utilizes pleasure to create joy and happiness. Pleasure is not an end in itself but a means to a greater end—happiness. Consider eating. The taste of good food is distinct pleasure, but it can be more than that. When eaten in the company of good friends, it becomes a sacrament of friendship; the meal becomes an occasion which good companionship makes enjoyable. When Jesus sat with His disciples to eat, He paused to give thanks to God. In that moment, the pleasure of eating became an experience of gratitude, it became a moment of inner joy through remembering that food is a gift of God's good earth, a symbol of His care.

Food eaten with thanksgiving is more than pleasure; it is an inner experience of faith, faith becoming confidence and trust, and inner peace of mind. You folk who set food before your children with never a word of thanks to God may be nourishing their bodies while starving their spirits. The same bowl of cereal which fills an empty stomach can, with a prayer of thanks, fill an empty soul with the joy of believing in God's care.

There is a beautiful story of Jesus attending a wedding. To the teetotaler, it is a perennial problem, while the imbiber quotes it to prove his right to indulge in drink. And both are mistaken. You remember, Christ provided the best wine for the celebration of the wedding, and it came after all the other was consumed. Have you wondered why the wine at all and why Jesus produced it so late in the feast?

The writer of this story knew human nature, and he also knew the problems which marriage can produce. To me, *the story of Christ at the wedding is a parable of how He elevates the pleasure of marriage to the level of enduring happiness, for wine is a symbol of joy.* In early stages of marriage, the pleasure of the relationship is sufficient to fulfill the expectations of both. But with the passing of time and the stress of tensions which develop between people, the law of diminishing returns begins to operate. It is then that the new wine of happiness must be added. It is then that the physical relationship of pleasure must be infused with the spiritual wine of love, true love, other-regarded love, love which places the joy of the mate above his own pleasure, love which treats the mate not as a thing to be used but as a person whose total being is to be loved and respected.

The physical experience of love then becomes a total experience of body and spirit, the love of the spirit, elevating the love of the body through pleasure that fades, to the joy of body *and* spirit that endures. *We discover then that happiness in marriage does not depend so much on the techniques of love as on the totality of love, in which body and soul are inseparably joined.*

The Christian faith again is adequate for the joys that invite us in that, while not ignoring the physical, directs us to put our emphasis on the mental and esthetic and spiritual in life. The person who takes this road to happiness is never dependent entirely on the circumstances of his life. He will find joy in the furnishings of his mind and spirit rather than of his office or home. William Lyon Phelps, beloved teacher of English Literature at Yale, knew of this when he said, "The happiest person is one who thinks the most interesting thoughts" and "A well-ordered life is like climbing a tower; the view halfway up is better than the view from the base, and it steadily becomes finer as the horizon expands."

The happy person is not a bored person, and boredom, an inner state of mind, is impossible to the well-stocked mind. Was this not what Jesus meant when He said that happy are the poor in spirit whose material wants are soon met. Happy are the pure in heart who think the best thoughts; happy are the meek who really possess the whole earth. *The beatitudes are clues to real happiness and joy.*

And in addition, it leads us into real happiness because it leads us out of too much self-preoccupation. When Jesus washed His disciples' feet as a symbol of service, He concluded, "If ye know these things, happy are ye if ye do them." For our service makes us worth something to someone, and there can be no happiness without that. John Burroughs knew this when he commented that real joy and happiness can only come from having something worthwhile to do. And a newspaper editor in Great Britain knew it when he asked readers to describe the happiest people they knew. The prize went to these: A craftsman whistling at work, a child building castles in the sand, a mother bathing her baby after her hard day's work is done, a doctor who has completed an operation, knowing he has helped to save a life. This is the way it works out. *If you are serious about the pursuit of happiness, try Christ's way.*

Thoughts on Collection Three

Childhood's Bill of Rights was an eye opener for me, in that it was one of the first times my grandfather was obviously forceful in his writing. He was not holding back at all when it came to his thoughts around the rights of children to family, love, and faith: The Big Three.

He was not holding back on his thoughts surrounding what happens to a child who is devoid of The Big Three. Those who are causing challenges for others in our world today, and sixty years ago, were most likely missing one of these elements at some point in their childhood. I certainly don't believe every malcontent in our world is suffering from a lack of these elements during their childhoods, but what could our world look like if we figured out how to give every kid a shot at a life with The Big Three, front and center?

Love is the answer here. If we love our children, won't we truly make sure these things are paramount to their lives? Won't we do all we can to help them discover the love residing in a mother's eyes for her infant? To me, that "mother's love" is the kind of love Jesus has for all of us. Think about it.

I can't go on about love without thinking through the second message in this collection. *For the Loneliness that Desolates Us* is so timely as we begin to again emerge from a world of lockdown. Seriously, loneliness is one of the biggest issues arising from the pandemic. It was a problem for people then, and it may be an even bigger problem today.

This message was delivered in the 1960s; imagine how much bigger the world is today? In the mid-1960s, the population of the world is estimated to have been about 3.2 billion. We're more than double that in 2022. And yet, with nearly 4 billion more people around us, we all still know people who are lonely.

It seems the cure is another sure-fire winner to me. The cure looks a whole lot like getting uncomfortable again, one person at a time. Making time to befriend someone, even just one, we may not know as well as we ought to. That person could be in an assisted-living center, in your office, in the pew in the back row, living in your house, riding on the train, anywhere. Truly.

Man, I cringe just thinking about it. But I know it's the way home. I know it's the right thing to do, both as a Christian and as a person. When I engage with people like this and show even the slightest hint of human kindness, God takes over. The light shines again. A smile can dash a thousand frowns and furrowed brows. Being intentional with someone who needs a friend *is* love. It's amazing love. It's part of becoming something better than ourselves, and it won't cost a thing, but it could help save someone's soul.

How did Grandpa say it again? *"Our faith insists that in all relationships concern for the other person is basic. This is the true meaning of love."*

Dang it, Grandpa.

As I come to a close on my final thoughts for this collection, *For the Joys that Invite Us* provides an amazing look into several kinds of happiness. It also pulls back the curtains to reveal the kind of love that leads to true happiness in marriage. I love it.

It's a reminder that pleasures of the senses will ultimately fade, but with intentional attentions as our core motivation, we can tap into an even greater level of happiness than we thought possible. Grandpa gets into those thoughts by again illustrating an act of Christ at the wedding. Old wine equals young love and the pleasures it holds. New wine equals enduring love and the joys and happiness it ultimately reveals via our intentionality toward our mate. Wow. That's good stuff in my book.

Even though Grandpa hit a home run with those analogies, I also want to shine a little light on my earthly father, James Delano LaRock. He was a man who happened to spend a little time with C. Maxwell Brown, his father-in-law, and no doubt learned a thing or two about intentional, right relationships with people via their time together.

I lost my dad during the writing of this book. He passed in March of 2022. He's home with God now, and I can safely say the process of his ascension to heaven was at times challenging yet also beautiful.

I was given the opportunity to talk a little more about it on a podcast recently, hosted by a friend of mine named Tom Henderson. The podcast is called the *ResGen Giving Life Podcast*, and I was honored to be invited to it to share some thoughts about the passing of loved ones and things of that nature.

If I'm any good at all at loving my wife, I owe that to God. And to my dad.

My dad was affectionately known as "Big Jim" in our family. He had an amazing way of loving my mother which rarely involved anything ornate or lavish. I watched him all of my years, even into my early fifties now, as he showed us how it looks to love intentionally. Here's a quick story…

In my childhood years, on most weekends, I would get up a little past nine o'clock (maybe ten) and watch some Saturday Morning Cartoons on TV, eat a little Captain Crunch, play some Atari and just hang out.

Around eleven o'clock or so, I would make my way upstairs to find my dad most often reading the newspaper in our living room. He had a favorite chair that sat right in front of a big window overlooking the backyard.

I'd go over and ask something like, "Dad, what are we gonna do today?"

"Danny," he'd reply, "I have no idea what we're going to do today, because your mother hasn't told me what I *want* to do yet today." And a sly grin would emerge on his face.

Then he'd go on, "When your mother tells me what I *want* to do today, then I will tell you what *you're* going to do today!"

This was a refrain so familiar, I practically walked into it every time. Just to see him smile about it.

He already knew Mom had a plan, or was in the middle of making one, but, truth be told, he didn't really care what we were doing on any given Saturday. He just wanted to be with her, with us, be a family. Moving together in rhythm, simply dancing through our days together.

That's how I first learned about the good that comes from putting the needs of others ahead of my own.

Thanks for sticking with me as I shared that story about my dad. It was really something to know him, and if you did, you know what I mean.

One of the curious things about Christianity, and one of the reasons I became even more drawn to it, is that it is based on the very real story of an enduring, intentional, sacrificial love for us from God, manifested through Christ. Within the realm of world religions, Christianity has a lot to say regarding the roles of family, faith and love in our world. And, because it does, I thought it was worth diving into a little deeper.

As we wrap up *Intentional Love in All Relationships*, I am not unaware that these first few collections of messages, and my associated thoughts, all presume a few things.

One, Christianity is Real.

Two, Christ Lived.

And three, because He lived, we have some work to do.

That's why this fourth section matters so much. Its focus is on history and Christian apologetics. My grandfather had plenty to say about the history of the faith, and honestly, this is an area where I find I spend a lot of time.

I needed to know where my faith came from. I needed to know that I could trust it as a bonafide guide for my life. I don't know why I like all the geeky apologetics stuff, but I do. Bear with me on this next collection; I truly hope it'll resonate with you enough to make you dive a little deeper into the history.

Keep reading, and hopefully you'll see what I mean.

COLLECTION FOUR

OH NO!
HISTORY MATTERS?!

Yes, it does.

In the following messages, my grandfather illustrates that going a little bit below the surface of the Christian faith is important because you can then discover its roots. He frequently refers to the history of the world, as told through the Bible, as the history of God interacting with people. Some of the stories in that history are incredible, some are confounding. All of them blend together to tell an incredibly diverse tale.

If you haven't spent much time in the Bible, I really hope you will start to incorporate it into a regular habit. It is, after all, a Habit that helps. If you do, you will no doubt find that there is absolutely nothing new under the sun. There are no stories in our modern world that haven't been told before. The Bible is rich with beauty, but also contains stories of incredible deception and destruction. It's a crazy book. And one I hope you will be inspired to read.

I remember the first time I was inspired to read the Bible, cover to cover. It was in 2007, and I was thirty-six. At the time, I was pretty consumed with my new job, our marriage, our kids and our family life. Suffice to say, I was busy! So, reading for enjoyment had definitely taken a backseat to the game of life.

The *Twilight* series of books had been released in 2005, and they were all the rage at the time. Somehow, while on a little getaway, my wife encouraged me to take up reading again and thought maybe those books could hold my attention. As it turned out, there were about fifty to seventy-five pages in each book that contained a ton of fighting and violent action and, if I'm honest, those parts were pretty good.

But the books themselves were like 500 pages each, and when I finally wrapped them up in 2008, I discovered I had consumed something like 2000 pages of romantic, love-struck vampires and werewolves all wrapped up into some kind of twisted, weird, monster loves monster fictional life that truly led nowhere. Again, there were about 250 pages of some serious fighting and suspenseful action, and, to me, those were OK.

It was right near the end of that series that I opened a Bible at church one morning—imagine that! And what did I discover? It was about 2000 pages long. The conviction hit me cold.

I thought, if I just spent two years reading 2000 pages of fictional monster romance, how on earth can I *not* spend the next two reading the story of God among people?

That did it for me. And, wow, it's been worth it. What'll it be for you?

Here's a little from Grandpa, circa fifty-seven years ago, on the subject.

You Can Find God in History

December 27, 1964

"For in Him we live, and move, and have our being…" Acts 17:28 (KJV)

During the week just past, hundreds of millions of people in all parts of the world paused to celebrate the birth anniversary of Jesus of Nazareth. On Friday night next, the world will turn in its old calendar and open a new one bearing the date in 1965. Doesn't it seem significant to you, as it surely does to me, that these two events, given such worldwide observance, are religious in their origin? We celebrate the birth anniversary of Jesus because for these many centuries he has been regarded by much of the world as the Son of God in a unique sense.

The year 1965 is the Year of our Lord, *Anno Domini*, 1965. We establish our calendars by reference to this birth. These are points in history. They represent an event in the life story of man, his story, which requires us, it seems, to spell it with a capital H, History, becoming in truth, "His" God's story also. For the story of man would have been tragically less inspiring, devoid of gentleness and bereft of hope had not His Story been woven into man's story, which we call history.

For those who are concerned to recover a sense of the reality of God, let me commend a reading of history as His Story. St. Paul, speaking of the intelligentsia of his day, the people of Athens, insisted that it was in God that we live and move and have our being. Living in Him, history is made to become "His story."

Could this be what H. G. Wells meant when he said that "Human history in essence is the history of ideas?" Or what Alfred North Whitehead meant when he insisted that history is determined in the "guts" of people, in other words the things that hurt them, their sense of outraged justice and what inspires them—their imperishable hopes! The history of the American Revolution didn't begin with the Boston Tea Party, or the shots heard round the world from Concord, Massachusetts. It began long before that in the hopes and dreams of men who believed they were, as sons of God, endowed with some inalienable rights. Having known the freedom of God's sons, they could not endure the tyranny of George III.

"In the beginning was the Logos," a Greek word, capable of several translations. In the beginning was the "Word." The idea, or plan, the word, was with God, and the word, idea, plan, was God. This word, idea, plan, became flesh and dwelt among us supremely in the person of Jesus of Nazareth. Yet God continues to become living flesh in the lives of all who believe in Him and respond to Him. God becomes actively involved in the very human affairs of men as he takes form in man's struggles for the fulfillment of His highest purposes.

We who profess to live by the teachings and insights of the Hebrew-Christian faith get our bearings from historic incidents in which we believe God was involved, and in which His involvement was a determinative factor. We cannot believe that man operates the world strictly on his own, that he is without responsibility to none but himself. Count Tolstoy in his *War and Peace* asserts properly, we think, that "If every man could act as he chose, the whole of history would be a tissue of disconnected accidents."[5]

We believe that the story of man indicates progress of man, not inevitable progress, but progress made when man is true to the great ideals which have become part of this heritage. *It is our belief that God acts in human history through the pull of those great dreams He has awakened in men's minds, through the authority of the truth which will not allow man to be long comfortable with falsehood.* The power of the "great lie" is a fabrication. It cannot endure. God, we believe, is involved in the human drama, by reason of the inescapable relationship of cause and consequences. *We are free to choose our acts but never free to choose the consequences of those acts.* The consequence is inherent in the act itself. To put it more succinctly, we believe in the power of the spirit, the spirit of God working through the spirit of man, illuminating, revealing, judging, inspiring, empowering man. We believe history is indeed His Story, too.

Let's see how it looks in actual human situations. The Bible is not a book of philosophy, but the record of events in which men and women considered themselves servants of the God of justice, mercy, truth, and love. And the character of their lives, the influence of their deeds, reflects the result of that belief. There is no other accounting for the Old Testament heroes, Moses and the Prophets; there is no accounting for the life and influence of Jesus Christ; nor the world-changing effect of those first disciples, of whom it was said, "those who are upsetting the world" have come. In retrospect, we observed them not upsetting the world but setting it right side up, where the truest values and the noblest purpose of man are given their rightful position.

We say of the Bible, that it is a book "inspired of God" meaning that those who lived and wrote were inspired by their relationship to God through faith in Him. *And the strange thing about it is that we do not need to defend them, or explain them, but only expose our minds and spirits to their life stories and we find ourselves likewise inspired.* The power of God recorded in the life of those men of Old becomes the inspiring power of men living in the year 1964. The most recent example, I suspect, is that of Doctor Paul Carlson[6], who, moved by his love of man and faith in God, stayed on to heal the sick and lost his life in the act. And who can measure the long-range results of that twentieth century martyrdom? It will be more than a date in the history of the Congo, for those who experienced the healing of his hand and heart will never be the same again.

You see, we have to make a choice here as everywhere. We can choose to read history as a series of events without any attempt to probe the motivations of men involved, and to understand the source of those motives, without which it does become a "tissue of disconnected accidents" or a "tale told by an idiot, full of sound and fury, signifying nothing."[7] Or we can read it and hear it with an open ear to the anguish and the hopes, the suffering and the anticipations of men and women in the act of making history. And, I am persuaded, this is the only meaningful way to understand the story of man. For man is a creature who thinks and feels and hopes and hurts.

Reading history as His Story is the only way I can be saved from utter despair. Reading between the lines and behind the lines I see the hand of God, and the story we hear is not the Babel of human voices only, but the voice of the God of justice still offering men the opportunity of repentance and reform.

I remember an event which took place in the year of 1954. It was in August of that year. A British passenger plane was shot down off the Island of Hainan, by planes from the Chinese mainland. American lives were lost. Before the incident was settled, American flyers had shot down two Chinese planes. The world held its breath, fearing this might be the spark to set off the explosion that would be World War III.

In that same month, August 1954, 125,000 people gathered in Soldiers Field, Chicago. They were there to attend an opening of the Second Assembly of the World Council of Churches. Standing at silent attention, these 125,000 heard Dr. Mark Boegner, President of the World Council, challenge them with this question, "Who are you who have come here?" The 125,000 replied in one voice, "We are Christians. We have come from many different traditions." And Dr. Boegner pressed on. "What is it to be Christian?" And they replied, "It is to believe in God the Father; in His Son Jesus Christ our Lord, who is the hope of the world, and in His Holy Spirit." "From where have you come?" inquired the President. "From a 161-member church from 48 countries and five continents," the people replied. And then the final question. "Why have you come?" And they replied, "We have come to worship God."

Both of these August events were history in the making. One with the possibility of blowing the world apart. The other with the power to bind the world together. And I believe firmly that the power of God working through those who worship Him in all nations of the world will eventually provide the way to which our broken humanity will find itself as a family of man, living together in mutual respect and harmony.

In the ancient prophecy of Isaiah, we read these words, "It shall come to pass in the last days, that the LORD's house shall be established in the top of the mountains... all nations shall flow unto it. And many people shall go and say, Come ye, and let us go up to the mountain of the LORD... and he will teach us of his ways, and we will walk in his paths: for out of Zion shall go forth the law, and the word of the LORD from Jerusalem. And he shall judge among the nations... and they shall beat their swords into plowshares, and their spears into pruning hooks: nation shall not lift up sword against nation, neither shall they learn war anymore." And in the final book of the Bible, we are given a picture of the New Jerusalem, the City of man become the City of God. This is the idea, the dream which the spirit of the God of truth and justice and love is leading us to realize.

It is never quite accurate to identify any existing institutions as the fulfillment of God's purposes, for, being human, they can and often do fall short. Yet we can see in our own time the beginnings of the realization of that dream. We see in the United Nations organization, a small beginning of a structure within which this diverse world with its many cultures may find a political basis for governing its affairs. Through our interchange of people, across all barriers and boundaries, we are beginning to exchange our prejudices for the truth about one another.

The very destructiveness of our modern weapons can, and I think must, be interpreted as God saying to the world, "The unity I have tried to help you develop through peaceful relationship, is now forced upon you by necessity. The law of consequences requires that you find nonviolent ways of settling your differences." Who can doubt that the great service agencies of the U.N., UNESCO, the World Health Organization, the Food and Agricultural Organization, are means to a noble end, the feeding of the hungry, the clothing of the naked, the healing of the sick, the enlightening of the ignorant and unlearned?

Some are disturbed that U.N. help goes to all people. Whether they agree with us or not. To me, it expresses the will of God, whose Son loved all men and died for all. Yes, God is at work in history. We need to read the story of man with eyes open to all the truth, and hearts responsive to the hope it reveals. Then we see the God of Truth, the God of Justice, the God of Love, the God of Life, working through men and women to achieve His holy purposes. Won't you see the story of man through the eyes of Christ, and of the followers of Christ? History then becomes "His Story."

The Greatest Story Ever Told

December 8, 1963

Everybody loves a story. It is one of the few points where people of diverse ages or points of view can meet. Witness a grandmother reading a story to her grandchild. A span of sixty years is no barrier when a story is told. A story bridges the gap not only between generations but between cultures. The greatest stories of all are translated into many languages, because they speak the universal language of human experience. During the childhood of our race, storytelling was a principal means for the transmission of cultural treasures from generation to generation. Stories gave a tribe or nation its character and thus its identity. More mature cultures still use the story in art forms of novel and drama, to convey much that can never be expressed in statistics or factual reports.

So, we ought not be surprised, but rather gratified, that our own culture has its roots firmly grounded in and nourished by the world's greatest stories. I speak of the Bible, of course. The Bible was spoken before it was written, and because of its poetic and dramatic story-form, still speaks, though written, to each generation in turn. And because it reflects the universal state of mankind, it speaks to men and women of the most diverse cultural backgrounds. It has been translated into over 1,000 languages and dialects and is, without question, the most widely read literature in the world.

I speak of the Bible as the greatest story ever told. I believe it can so qualify by every standard of judgment. For instance, the most popular form of the story follows this pattern. It begins in hope and happiness, followed by tragedy. It relates human effort to recover, but failure continues. Then the rescuer appears, and the end is final triumph of right, and happiness ever after. This is the format of the fairy tale, of great drama, of inspiring biography. In fact, historic epochs are reported on that plan, such as the story of our own nation. It is the format of your life story and mine—great hope, failure, struggle, rescue and then success and happiness. The Bible story begins in the Garden of Eden, a garden of happiness and hope. Comes the fall of man and his expulsion from this hope and happiness—the tragic element. Follows the centuries of struggle, always ending in failure. Came finally the deliverer, Jesus of Nazareth, and the restoration of hope and happiness, called the Kingdom of God.

The greatness of this story is seen again in the variety of its literary forms. One finds within its covers some of the world's matchless poetry, the Psalms. One finds some of the world's most profound myths. The Tower of Babel story is an illustration. There is history here, the story of a nation's search for its own character and identity, its struggles, its failures, its victories, but always, too, its faith. *For this is the history of people working out their faith in the rough and tumble of life.* There are love stories here, there is biography here, the story of men and women who, to use Pascal's phrase, are the "glory and the scandal of the universe." *There is scandal. No sin that man ever conceived or practiced is ignored here.*

Bishop Kennedy once commented that "All the betrayals of the soul, the lusts of the flesh and the evils of the spirit are confronted in the Bible. So much of the shocking descriptions of modern literature appears to be like small boys writing bad words on walls than an honest revelation of human nature. But the Bible dares to begin with the worst and look into the dark places of the human soul." But the scandals of the Bible are more than matched with the glories of man—man the pioneer, man the law giver, man the organizer, man the dreamer, man the builder, man the poet, man the dramatist, man the parent, and supremely, man, the revealer of the eternal love and truth which is God. What an impoverished world this would be without the great personalities of Abraham, Moses, David, Isaiah, Amos, Jeremiah, Ruth, Mary, Peter, and Paul, but supremely, Jesus of Nazareth. All of them are given the world through the pages of the Holy Bible. Yet, with all this, it is a story that is not read as it deserves to be. For many of us, our acquaintance with it is through the Hollywood distortions of its great epics and personalities. And why? Well, perhaps we are lazy and don't like to read. But more likely it is because we have forgotten to read it as a great story and let it speak to our imaginations.

Perhaps the Church is at fault here, when it sets out to make every line and paragraph yield something fundamental and profound. Perhaps our own state of mind these days works against us. We may have approached it with a fact-finding motive, due to our belief that science is our salvation. So, when we read the creation stories, and that God created the universe in six days, we know it was not done in six days of twenty-four hours each, so we lay it all aside as false and mere fabrication.

Or when we read that Moses saw a bush burning that was not consumed and heard the voice of God from the bush, we decided that since bushes are consumed when they burn, Moses most certainly did not hear the voice of God. And when we read the story of Jonah, we are tempted to make the credibility of the prophecy depend on the edibility of the prophet. *We have missed the point of so much of the Bible because we have not read it as story revealing the deep and life transforming experience of man, a clue to the same life transforming power which awaits each of us if we will.*

But let's get back to the Bible story itself. It begins in a garden with everything designed for man's happiness. It begins as every man's life begins, in a state of innocence when he knows neither good nor evil. This is the innocence of childhood. But, as everyone listening to my voice knows, the age of innocence does not last. A child learns, he eats of the tree of knowledge and discovers the difference between right and wrong. He is then expelled from the garden of innocence. The Bible says a flaming sword keeps him from returning. And we know that we can't go back into innocency.

One can't unlearn what he knows. One can't cut himself off from his primitive ancestry. Our past is always a part of any present moment. The Bible calls this the fall of man. Well, from then on out, Biblical man is struggling with this past, trying to keep it under control and finding that it is impossible. The story is the record of man's attempt to save himself from this inner conflict. Our forefathers called this past man's "carnal nature." *One can identify some rare qualities in his being if he is honest—a bit of the tiger, too much of the ape, a generous endowment of the parrot, and what of the peacock, and the stubborn mule. I can see a bit of all of these anytime I look into the mirror of my soul.*

Freud did us a great service in helping us know something of the complexity of our racial heritage. Man is in search of his own individual identity. His varied powers seek to serve his ego, his "I" if you please, so necessary if he is to be an individual. Yet man cannot be man alone—he must also live in relation to others and here the trouble begins. The Bible story has Eve as the source of trouble, not because she was a woman but because she was another person. Conflict of interest? Just read your daily paper for the latest record of this struggle. We can't retreat into ignorance and innocence. We must be individuals with driving ego needs. We must also be social beings relating to each other. It is an impossible situation, isn't it? Yet here we are. Man is Humpty Dumpty, who had a great fall, and all the king's horses can't seem to put him back together properly.

The Bible relates how many ways man has tried. The Prophet said, "Repent, change your mind, stop doing wrong." But what does one do with the submerged set of drives below the threshold of awareness and not amenable to one's willpower? The Priest said, "Make some sacrifices." If your sin costs you enough, you will decide it isn't worth the price. But we find that even capital punishment doesn't stop some folk. Some of us try the sacrifice method, psychologists call it compensation. The Bible, which tries to free us from the burden of compensation, asks, "And what does the LORD require of you? But to do justly, to love mercy, and to walk humbly with our God?" Well and good, but who can do it?

So, next, man constructed laws by which he can define his responsibilities. In the keeping of the rules, it is hoped that man can be both an individual and a socially fulfilled person. But the proliferation of laws is just another kind of slavery and man is born to be free. Totalitarian governments of the twentieth century think they can revert to this ancient and thoroughly discredited form of social organization.

Now, all do help a bit; the Prophet's word to repent and cease does help. The sacrifice motif of "compensation" will help to some extent. Certainly, laws are needed to give us some guideposts, some limits to our personal freedom. But through all of this man has retained in his memory, too, this edge of innocency. We see in ourselves some reflection of the Divine freedom, some intimations of the immortal, and all devices which man has contrived to recapture that image and that freedom have failed. So, he struggles on, often in failure, always a bit unhappily.

Now we have in our story, hope, disaster, struggle, failure. What of the deliverer?

The Christian hails his coming at Christmas time, "… Unto you is born this day… a Saviour, which is Christ the Lord." And Jesus came, to do what? To reconcile us to God, to ourselves and to one another. He does not offer man a retreat into innocence. He knows the clock won't turn back. In the place of innocence, he offers forgiveness, which is just this: *Man the individual becoming man in relationship, made possible by the Love which accepts one just as he is.* And in this relationship of love, one finds to his joy that he is not in competition but in fellowship. His ego drives bring him to fulfillment in the fellowship of God who forgives and with God's family which also forgives and receives him.

Here is the return of hope and joy and promise through love, for to the Christians, God is love and all love is of God. This deliverance Christ came to give us, and with it, the Kingdom of God, a new life for a renewed humanity. And so Christians sing with feeling and faith, "All hail the power of Jesus' name, let angels prostrate fall. Bring forth the royal diadem and crown Him Lord of all." For the Christian, Christ is Lord. And in surrender to his Lordship, man finds not innocency but forgiveness and fellowship and life at its joyful best. This is the story. Hope, tragedy, struggle, failure, deliverance and happiness ever after. *Yes, it's the greatest story ever told, but do you know that story's meaning in your life?*

The God Who Intervenes

August 4, 1963

In the year 1732, the people of Paris were awed and excited by reports that miracles were taking place in and about the St. Medard Cemetery. So troublesome did the excited people become, that Louis 15th locked the gates of the cemetery and posted this sign: "By order of the King, God is hereby forbidden to work miracles in this place."

We are first amused and then perhaps a bit repelled by such arrogance. Is it the prerogative of kings to give orders to God? Yet in our own time we have similar signs posted all over our universe by men who, having been impressed with the orderliness of it all, have decided that any intervention by a Divine Spirit is impossible. We, in our time, have become so impressed with the laws of the universe, and rightly so, that we have, not so rightly perhaps, forgotten that there may also be a Law-Giver in the universe.

A consequence of this is a drift away from the religion of the scriptures. For a great many people, even in our Christian churches, religious faith has become a regard for what they feel to be the moral law of the world we live in, and in practice, a broad humanitarianism based on the more easily accepted teachings of Jesus. This brand of faith, though not wrong in itself, suffers severe limitations as religious faith.

The religion taught in both the Old and New Testaments, presumably the source of our faith, not only requires reverence for the moral law and commands humanitarianism concern, it adds another factor which makes it a dynamic faith, namely belief in a God *who is active in human affairs.* And there is a basic difference between faith in a God who intervenes and faith in impersonal law, immutable but unknowing.

The first invites us to a joint endeavor with God in a purpose of His choice, in which He is actively engaged. Man working in league with God remembers that he does not struggle alone. He draws his courage and his stamina from this firm conviction. The concept of God as impersonal law may leave man in despair when his best efforts seem to fail. I expect our difficulty with the thought of God who intervenes grows out of the rather generally accepted notion that God intervenes by temporarily suspending the operation of natural laws. Biblical stories of the Red Sea rolling back or the sun standing still for the convenience of God's people just won't do for our time. Perhaps what we need to do is to ask, just how does God intervene in man's life, granted that He does?

Well, the Bible teaches us that *God is a spirit. And in His dealings with man, intervening if you will in man's life, He makes his contact with us through our spirit.* Let us see how this may come about.

Consider, for instance, this. The human race turned a corner in its long trek toward a life organized around high ethical requirements, at the time of Abram. Abram lived in Ur of the Chaldees. But on a day, or series of days, he experienced an inner impulse and illumination or inspiration. It seemed to him that if he left the culture in which he grew up and moved to another land, obeying meanwhile this inner voice, following this inner light, then he might well become the founder of a new nation, and this nation would take its character, not from the strength of its armies, but from its loyalty to the God who inspires and who makes high ethical demands upon His people.

The glorious fact is that Abram sold his holding and, as the Bible says, "… went out, not knowing whither he went." You see, here is a religion of adventure, with its face always to the future. Here is religion, growing out of faith in God, who keeps His believing people faced forever toward new adventures in human relationships, toward higher reaches of ethical responsibility. Explain as we will what happened in the life of Abram, from a source deep within and far beyond his social background came a voice that commanded his attention. And Abram obeyed. It is worth noting that it was this faith in a God who inspires, who commands and who leads out into the future, which flowed finally in the life of Jesus of Nazareth.

Take another illustration. The day came in the life of Abram when he abandoned the ancient rite of child sacrifice, leaving behind a reminder of the depth from which man has climbed. I should say *some* people have left it behind, for even in America children are sacrificed in some instances to their parents' self-interest. But Abram, nurtured in the practice of child sacrifice, found himself in a dilemma. He had been led to believe that he was to be the founder of a new nation. He had one child, Isaac. From far back in Abram's consciousness, probably, came the belief that this new God, whom he followed, now demanded the life of this son as a test of his own devotion.

From this incident has come one of literature's most fascinating stories. In the throes of Abram's agony, God again disclosed to him that his new faith was to lead him not only into new geography but new human relationships. Instead of his son, a lamb was provided for sacrifice, *the Bible's dramatic way of saying that our sacrifices must always be the wealth of our hands, not the product of our bodies and souls.* Some very modern men are not willing yet to accept this, where they prefer to send their sons to war rather than to pay the price of human well-being from the wealth of treasuries. Here is God, intervening in man's life to break inhuman and discredited patterns of human relationship. Here is God breaking into the stream of life to pull rather than push man up another step in his climb toward true humanity.

The life of Moses is another dramatic illustration. The followers of Abraham were now slaves in Egypt. A baby is born, a boy, and to save his life he is hidden from the authorities who were ordered to destroy Israel's babies because these slaves were outnumbering their Egyptian owners. Found by the Pharaoh's daughter, he was reared as a child of the palace, but nursed by his own mother, you remember. And here God's reach into the human soul is provided through that faithful mother, so that when the time of testing came, Moses knew he was a worshipper of the God of his fathers.

Don Marquis, in his magnificent poem about Moses, pictures him standing on the temple roof debating with himself as to his future. Below him spread the empire that would one day be his to rule, but that was not all.

> For one eternal instant Moses stood
> The cup of empire lifted to his lips...
> But overhead, a God.[8]

And in that moment, God won, and Moses lowered the cup of empire from his lips and descended from the temple roof, taking himself to the slave quarters "to lead them, if he might, from bondage."

God had intervened again by challenging the conscience and then the total life of a man who was to become a great emancipator, leading this nation of slaves out of their slavery into freedom. And in this state of political freedom, they were saved from anarchy by recognizing that they were to be governed by God. During this stressful but creative period, they developed a system of law which has come down to our own time in substance.

Part of it we call the Decalogue, the Ten Commandments. It was this which Hitler knew hampered severely his struggle for world power. So, he insisted that his German people be rid of what he called "this slave morality, this curse of Mount Sinai."

Yes, wherever His ethical standards challenge men and women, God still intervenes to modify and mold the life of the human race.

Take one more illustration from history, for the Scripture is in part history, the record of God's dealings with man. We celebrate this historic event at Christmas time. Here was the little nation of Israel ground under the heel of a ruthless military dictatorship. Living largely on a hope born of faith in a promised deliverer, she kept her weekly tryst with God in synagogue and temple. And then, on a silent night which to all Christians has become a Holy Night, a wondrous gift was given. Allowing for all the beautiful details which may have been read back into the story of Jesus' birth, we recognize that they are reverent attempts to account for the life of this One who seems to escape our normal human categories, to occupy a unique position in the human family as the Lord and Master of our spirits. Try as we may, we can't quite make him fit anywhere else. Listen to one great historian, Philip Schaff, as he talks about Jesus of Nazareth.

> This Jesus of Nazareth, without money and arms, conquered more millions than Alexander, Caesar, Mohammed and Napoleon, (and we might add Hitler or Stalin); without science or learning he shed more light on things human and divine than all scholars and philosophers combined; without the eloquence of schools he spoke such words of life as were never spoken before nor since, and produced effects which lie beyond the reach of orator or poet; without writing a single line, he set more pens in motion, and furnished themes for more sermons, orations, discussions, works of art, learned volumes, and sweet songs of praise than the whole army of great men of ancient and modern times. Born in a manger, and crucified as a malefactor, he now controls the destiny of the civilized world, and rules a spiritual empire embracing a third of the inhabitants of the globe.[9]

To those in our own time who know him, He is to the confused a light to guide them through their confusion, to the lonely he is a friend to trust; to the defeated, he is a source of renewing power, to the dying he is a promise that "life is real, life is earnest, and the grave is not its goal." Upon all our sins of body and spirit He sits in kindly but firm judgment by reason of His own sinlessness.

For all our failures He offers forgiveness and a new opportunity. To those who know Him best, He is what one called Him a long time ago, "Immanuel, God with us." Differ as we may about how He *came* to be we cannot account for what He *was* and what He *did* as just another normal human being. He lifts our sights so high, that we find it easy to say, "Surely this one is the son of God." In Jesus of Nazareth, we firmly believe that God intervened in human history by giving us, in human form, a definition of His own spirit, a delineation of His hopes for mankind, an invitation to

Collection Four: The God Who Intervenes

step up to a new level of personal and social living. *And since we know about Him, we cannot avoid doing something about Him. Whether we follow Him or deliberately ignore Him, God has intervened in our lives by requiring us to choose.*

To someone hearing my voice today, the thought doubtless occurs, "All you say may be convincing to one who accepts the Bible verbatim, but what of me, who must take all religious literature as a blend of fact and fancy, an interpretation of experience by men who look at the world through different eyes than mine?" Well, let's leave the Scriptures for a moment. Dean Lynn Harold Hough, a former teacher of mine, once called the natural laws the "habits of God." If we think of God as creator of the physical universe, then how better could we say it? The laws of nature are the way God acts through His creation habitually. And if this be so, then God intervenes in our daily lives each time we accommodate ourselves to the operation of these laws.

Or try another approach. A twentieth-century French scholar, Jack Maritain, put it this way. "Faith is participation in the knowledge of God. Charity is participation in the love of God." I like that. We Christians speak of God as the spirit of love and truth, because love and truth are the great creative and stabilizing powers in human relationships. Falsehood undermines, truth builds up. Hatred destroys life, love creates life. Falsehood and hatred may destroy the world. Truth expressed in love can redeem the world.

God is the spirit of truth and love, the one who creates and redeems the world; any human spirit which hungers for truth hungers for God. Any mind which grasps truth experiences God. Any man who experiences love, knows God. Any person who expresses love, serves God. It was said of Jesus "… we beheld his glory… full of grace and truth." So, Christ becomes to us the Way by which we come to God, and through whom God comes to intervene in our lives.

Well, what does this mean to you and me? Precisely this, that neither you nor I, nor any man, need live his life without the help of God. Our capacity to understand truth and to express love is our capacity to respond to God. *But what does it require of us? Just this—that we give Him some time and attention, for God meets us in our own spirits, where we think and feel and will and dream and hope and believe.* When we give Him our attention, He meets us in our own spirits, intervening creatively in our lives. If we take no time for worship, no time for study, if we remove ourselves from His influence by ignoring Him, He becomes unreal to us, and we are left to our own devices. God is as near as our thoughts. He waits to intervene on our behalf, and for our good.

Thoughts on Collection Four

I've read the Bible more than four times now. And I've hit the New Testament a few more times than that. Not a brag. At all.

It's something I've disciplined myself to do. Why? Each time, it gets more and more interesting. I find I am more and more engaged and less distracted by the long, "boring" parts. Even all the lists of names I can't pronounce.

I have become more interested in both the archaeology and the anthropology of the times in which these stories were happening and have found resources suitable to feed my interest. The more time I spend in it, the more I realize just how incredible *His-Story* has become. This is what most impacted me when I read *You Can Find God in History*.

I think about Jesus. His work. His walk. His time with people. His time healing people—literally *and* figuratively. His commitment to living for God. His acceptance of His time and place in history. His acceptance of God's will. All of it. It's truly amazing.

And He was Real. It isn't fiction.

On top of it, His Life inspired the men and women who became the first church. Some of them were martyred for what they knew to be true—because they'd seen it. Lived it with Jesus. Crazy. These are the things I began to think more about and what drew me to *The Greatest Story Ever Told*.

But His life and their lives led to the creation of so much of what our world recognizes as "good" today.

As Grandpa, quoting Philip Schaff, wrote, Jesus, "*without writing a single line, set more pens in motion, and furnished themes for more sermons, orations, discussions, works of art, learned volumes, and sweet songs of praise than the whole army of great men* (trillions) *of ancient and modern times.*"

Really think about that. Marinate in it.

So, I'm extremely nerdy about Christian apologetics. What exactly does that mean and how do I define it?

Christian apologetics can be summarized in two parts: (a) objective reasons and evidence that Christianity is true (Jesus lived) and, (b) the patient and compassionate communication of that truth to the world.

The earliest Christian believers were Jews, and so, ironically, the earliest Christian apologists were also Jews. Two-thousand plus years ago, as they shared their new faith in Christ to their Jewish families and friends, they appealed primarily to the Old Testament and to Jesus' bodily resurrection as the primary evidence for belief in Christ.

Today, Christian apologists engage with philosophies and ideologies such as naturalism, atheism, pantheism, post-modernism and humanism. These philosophies, of course, also include Darwinism.

OK, so that's all a little bit nerdy, right?!

It is, but it also helps me understand so many of the foundations, mostly good, some challenging, for much of the world in which we live. And, certainly, in the Western Hemisphere.

What do I mean?

Jesus lived. His life meant something. He came to Earth to show us a better way to be in relationship with each other. A better way to work with each other. As people. It was revolutionary. Most atheists will even admit that.

Jesus. Was. Different.

And, His life, death and resurrection *inspired* a revolution of thought, being and human existence.

So, there's that.

And then there's the very foundations of living upon which our lives revolve.

Human Rights.
Healthcare.
Universities.
Western Law.
Freedom.
Charity.

Each of these fundamental components of our lives are what they are today due to Christianity and its influence upon the human beings who ultimately were either exclusively or among the very first to develop each one.

First, these were ideas. Then, they became movements. And, ultimately, they are now bedrocks of our society. And they each trace their roots to Christians.

These each deserve far more time to explain than I will take here. And frankly, I am ill-equipped to provide written justice (there's another one) to any of them.

My thoughts have been influenced by many authors and historians, however. Folks far more intelligent and researched than I am. They include people like my grandfather and his words we've been exploring throughout this book.

I've also leaned into both old and new readings like *A Little History of the World* by E.H. Gombrich, *Dominion* by Tom Holland, *Bullies & Saints* by John Dickson, *UnBelievable*, by Justin Brierley and, recently, *The Fate of the Apostles* by Sean McDowell.

I have new ones on my list as well. I'll share many of them, and other resources I like in this area, at the conclusion of the book.

Overall, my life is simply much richer because of the time I've taken to really understand the evidence for my faith and, in turn, stumble and bumble my way into sharing it with others, patiently. That's why, in *The God Who Intervenes*, I stopped and highlighted these words: "*And since we know about Him, we cannot avoid doing something about Him.*"

Turns out, things go better with a little Jesus in them. People are better, too. I honestly struggle to explain all of it, but for me, it just works. Even the really, really tough stuff. Better. With. Jesus.

There is and there will no doubt always be suffering in the world. I am not qualified to dive deep here at all. There are many helpful, thought-provoking books written on this subject in particular. I encourage you to investigate.

All I can offer here on suffering is that perhaps God is hoping horrible circumstances like concentration camps, genocides, racial injustice and even George Floyd will wake us up permanently to the idea that our ways, which manifest themselves as control and Pharisaical righteousness, will never lead to beneficial relationships between people of different cultures.

Our ways will lead to the problems that Jesus came to help us solve. When we're paying attention and walking with Him, it's better. Not always perfect. Just better.

When we listen to ourselves, well, we can experience horrible abominations.

So, where do we go from here? What does a future look like when I've been paying more attention to the things of God? Are there basic truths we can pull from all of this?

Spending more time in The Bible is a great place to start. I've heard the following a few times, but it provides a really easy-to-digest thought about the book: **B**asic **I**nstructions **B**efore **L**eaving **E**arth

Clever, huh? Let's take a look at a possible future when things are better than they are today. Even when Ecclesiastes declares that there's "nothing new under the sun," there truly are better ways to deal with all the junk of life.

COLLECTION FIVE

WHAT ABOUT THE FUTURE?

So, where do we go from here?

Do we want the next sixty years to look like they do today?

How about the way we looked in the mid-1960s?

There's so much that's good in our world, but we've still got our problems. And real change takes a long, long time.

But my Grandpa Max had solutions for us back then, and they're not new. They're ripped from the pages of the Bible.

If we don't want the 2080s, to look like the 2020s, maybe we should consider deploying the advice from Grandpa's 1960s—try a little harder to link arms with Jesus.

Maybe try to, "chase the favor of God?"

These next messages offer both Hope and Ideas. I truly don't think any of us are that far away from making the difference that will enable the future to be brighter and better. I was filled with optimism reading them for the first time, but also felt challenged.

They made me think. Ponder. Helped me to commit to being more engaged. They helped me see that we can thrive in a future free of the guilt of past mistakes, while following the gentle influences of He who cares for us. Ultimately, we can live in the Hope we have all been craving for so long. It's real. It's available.

I hope you can see it, too.

For The Guilt That Haunts Us

September 1, 1963

"*For God sent not his Son into the world to condemn the world; but that the world through him might be saved.*" John 3:17 (KJV)

I.

Do you remember, as a child, your fascination with haunted houses? More than half afraid of them, we felt drawn to them, and, often with rapidly beating hearts, we stole through the emptiness of deserted rooms. We anticipated and at the same time feared what we might find. And always, we came away quietly and a bit awed, but never having found the occupant. After a while, we came to realize that houses are haunted for those for whom they hold some memories.

Sometimes the memories are hauntingly beautiful, but most often that which lingers is the memory of sorrow, or fear or failure. For it seems to be a trait of mankind that the unpleasant experiences burn themselves deepest into our memories. And so, our houses of memory are haunted with that which disturbs and accuses us.

And so all of us really live in haunted houses, for all of us live in the house of memory. And our memories are a mixture of the pleasant and the unpleasant. Each day becomes, living as we do in the world of the present and the past all mixed together, a struggle to break away from that haunting past. This spectre which dogs our path we call guilt, for it seems to remind us that, had we done differently, life would have been different and better.

So, we look to religion for an escape from this haunting presence. *And sometimes we find help in our religion as we have a right to expect. Sometimes we don't, and then we conclude that somewhere our religion has proven inadequate. For if we are to have an adequate religion, it must be one which helps us handle the guilt which so constantly haunts us.*

And the Christian faith is that kind of religion if we understand it correctly. The central statement of the faith is that which we learned as a child. "For God so loved the world, that he gave his only begotten Son, that whosoever believeth in him should not perish, but have everlasting life. For God sent not his Son into the world to condemn the world; but that the world through him might be saved." Does your religion do this for you, help you handle the guilt that haunts you? It can and should.

II.

An adequate religion such as the Christian faith helps us to handle our guilt by helping us first to locate the source of it. We find the condemning presence of some guilt haunting our memories. But how does it get there to begin with? Now, self-knowledge is only one step on the road to deliverance, but a necessary one. And Christ helps us to know the source of our guilt by helping us understand *who* we are, and *how* we are, *what* we are doing and *why*.

Often our feelings of guilt are undefined, in that they do not refer back to any specific act which in memory condemns us. It is rather a vague feeling of unworthiness, a constant attitude of self-reproach. Such feelings lie too deep to identify and thus are too vague for a specific handling. It is this which leads us to believe that part of our guilt lies in what we *are* rather than in what we *do*. We are created, it seems, with the capacity to "image

God" or reflect that which we conceive to be God, the highest and holiest we know.

This vague but constant feeling of guilt is reflected in the General Confession, as it says, "We have left undone those things we ought to have done; And we have done those things which we ought not to have done..."[10] We don't specify because we can't. Yet there is that overshadowing sense of failure. This must be the condition which inspired the scriptural idea of man's original sin, not something specific but a *constant* in his makeup.

Perhaps we can illustrate it in this way. Many of us as Americans have a sense of guilt because we are *white* Americans. Perhaps some folk of more deeply pigmented skin have a sense of guilt because they are darker, and in neither case is it a choice. Our very state involves us in a living situation which brings us into conflict and thus into guilt. *Perhaps by our very humanity, the fact that we are both animal and spirit, that we live in the tension of a dual being with the necessity of making ethical judgments by our nature, we are often under a sense of general condemnation.*

Perhaps the swing between our desire for spiritual autonomy and our desire for the irresponsibility which an animal existence would give us may account for our general guilt. But whatever its source, it is there, and we are the uneasy creatures of this earth. All men, of whatever culture, struggle with this sense of guilt, it seems, for all cultures provide some means of atoning for what man considers his sins.

Then, of course, as Christians we are exposed to a way of life, which by its very superiority is a source of condemnation for us. This is not intended in the Gospels, but it is a side effect which we suffer, though we ought not.

Do you remember in Shakespeare's *Othello* when Iago says of Cassio, "He hath a daily beauty in his life that makes me ugly"?[11] Just so, we who profess to be followers of Christ, find ourselves confronted daily with the beauty of person that was Jesus and are moved thus to feelings of guilt by a contrast we cannot escape. We have all read the "Sermon on the Mount" and probably, as we did, we have said within ourselves, "How idealistic and how impossible this really is!" Yet we cannot read the sermon and confront Christ without that contrast becoming a source of condemnation to us.

Fritz Kreisler died a year ago, bringing to a close the life of one of the world's foremost violinists. In a series of articles about him, another of

Collection Five: For The Guilt That Haunts Us

America's violinists said this, "I heard Kreisler one day when I was a young man. I determined that day to give my life to the violin. But that was only a beginning." One can imagine the days and nights of practice, the days of self-recrimination when he failed to play as Kreisler played. Then, perhaps, the day came when he discovered that he was not to play as Kreisler played, but to play *his* best, under the inspiration of a greater one than he. And his guilt was gone. Only the inspiration remained. So it is in our relation to Christ. We are *judged* and *inspired* but *not condemned.*

The Christian faith is one which does indeed produce feelings of guilt, but at the very moment it introduces us to the One who saves us from our guilt while continuing to keep us reaching for the higher levels of thought and conduct. *It is a religion destined for men and women who will not settle for less than the best in themselves.* Let's see how adequate it is for the guilt that haunts us.

Our faith is adequate because it refuses to let us escape failure through projecting our guilt to another and thereby condemning it. Thus, it is a common device of people. The Old Testament story of Adam and Eve is a classic example of passing the buck. Adam blamed his wife, Eve, and Eve said no, it was the snake that beguiled me. And no one was the better nor wiser for that. The greedy man is most likely to condemn greed in another, for this device saves him from acknowledging his own greed. The lewd man is most aware of lewdness in others, if for no other reason than he is looking for it. And he, too, is prone to condemn in another what he finds discreditable in himself. No, Christ calls us to repentance of our own sins, not to thus add guilt to failure, but to turn failure into achievement. Only as we acknowledge today's failure will we be instructed in how to make tomorrow a better day.

Again, the Christian faith saves us by refusing to let us forget our faults and again slip into patterns of failure. This too, is a common device to escape guilt without genuine correction of our failures. In the movie, *Good Morning, Miss Dove*, the heroine, Miss Dove, is in the hospital. Her pastor calls and suggests he might read for her the General Confession, which she could thus make her prayer of contrition. She replied, "No, don't read it. I have not done those things I ought not to have done, and I have not left undone what I ought to have done." As though ignoring the failure would erase its effects. She was unwilling to face her failure, ignoring the fact that her sin had not only infected her own life consciously and subconsciously, but also had infected her relationship. It is said that, in the eighteenth century, Lady Montague of London refused to look in the mirror for eleven years, since she did not want to be reminded that she was growing older and showing it. But it didn't change the fact.

No, Christ calls us to expose ourselves to judgment regularly in worship. When confronting Him, we know ourselves as needy people.

Finally, our faith does not relieve us of guilt falsely by encouraging us to adopt low standards of personal and social life. This means progressive deterioration of personal and social life. *The sensitivity of our conscience is the gauge of our growth. It measures our spiritual stature. Low standards may mean less guilt, to be sure, but it is the comfort of death, not the joy of life.* When Father Damien, who had worked among the lepers for years, accidentally spilled boiling water on his foot and felt no pain, he did not congratulate himself that he was immune to pain. He knew in that moment that he, too had become a leper, that death had set in. So with our consciences. *A quiet conscience may mean not freed from guilt but spiritual death.*

I am convinced that the Christian faith is made to order for man. It calls him to a high endeavor. Then it offers him forgiveness when he fails. It erases the guilt from his memory, setting him free in his climb toward the true manhood. *No, we need not live in houses haunted with the memories of past failure, but made light with the assurance of forgiveness, and brightened with the remembrances of weakness overcome.* It assures us that in spite of everything we are sons and daughters of God. Always remember that "If we confess our sins, [God] is faithful and just to forgive us our sins, and to cleanse us from all unrighteousness." Here is a religion adequate for the guilt that haunts us. Let us Pray.

> Oh God, in whom we live and move and have our being, enable us to feel the strength that surrounds us, to follow the light that indwells us, and to avail ourselves of the wisdom Thou givest liberally to all who ask of Thee. Give us so great a love of truth that we may pass beyond all doubt and error, until our minds are stayed on thee, and

our thoughts are kept in perfect peace. Give us the wisdom to follow the promptings of duty in our daily lives, that we may grow conscious of Thy presence who callest us to be fellow workers with Thee. Grant us the grace of penitence that we may not grow insensible of our need of forgiveness, from one another and from Thee; but seek cleansing in communion, fellowship in the light, and rest upon Thy heart. Amen.

God Commands – But Gently

August 18th, 1963

"... *Thou shalt love...* " Luke 10:27 (KJV)

All of us gladly acknowledge our debt to the man who gives us the right answers to our persistent questionings. The right answer to the question "What's wrong with me, Doctor?" may mean better health and longer life. The right answer to the question of how natural laws operate brings nature to our service. But our greatest debt is owed to the man who is wise enough to ask the right questions.

Right answers to wrong questions can still leave us wandering in ignorance and may be just as disastrous as the wrong answer to the right question. It takes as wise a man to ask the right question as to give the right answer. Most of us, I suspect, fail here. We spend too much attention on the wrong questions, like what shall we eat, or wear, what shall we do next for kicks. For most Americans, these are not the *really* important questions.

We owe a great debt to the man who asked this question: "What must I do to inherit eternal life?" And, interestingly enough, he was a man trained to ask the right question. He was a lawyer. Lawyers, you know, must develop skill in asking the right questions. Sometimes it is a loaded question, intended to trap a skittish witness into saying more than he intends. Sometimes it's a leading question, the answer to which will carry the case inevitably to the next question.

The lawyer in the story set out to trap Jesus with a loaded question. "Good master," he said, "what must *I*"—a lawyer, a professional man, a well-instructed member of the Hebrew faith—"What must *I* do to inherit eternal life?" And Jesus, being the master teacher that he was, didn't give him a dogmatic answer. He led him to discover his own answer by asking another question, in this case a leading question. "How do you read it in your law? What do you think is the answer?" And the lawyer replied, "Thou shalt love the Lord thy God with all thy heart, and with all thy soul, and with all thy strength, and with all thy mind; and thy neighbor as thyself."

Jesus then replied, "Thou hast answered right: this do, and thou shalt live." And then the lawyer, still trying, I think, to trap Jesus, came back with another loaded question, "And who is my neighbor?" That's the sticky one, isn't it? But it turned out to be a leading question, for it was Jesus' opening to tell a story, one of the most famous in all literature. We call it the story of the Good Samaritan. But Jesus told it to answer the question, "Who is my neighbor, and what does it mean to love him?" And note, if you will, that this matter is so basic to human life, that it is not offered as a suggestion, it is given as a commandment. "Thou shalt love."

If you want to live, then begin to look. It is God, who knows our nature and our needs, who commands, though gently, "Thou shalt love." And commands are meant to be obeyed, not debated, for a command at a critical moment may mean the difference between life and death. And, in this respect, this *is* that critical moment, for we are dealing with life and death each day that passes.

And this word is given in the imperative voice, a command, simply because our life as human beings depends upon our obedience to it. It is a *law of our existence*. Joshua Loth Leibman wrote what I think was one of the first, and probably the best, of a spate of books on the subject, *Peace of Mind*. In it, he makes this statement: "Everywhere we turn in the laboratory, whether in physics or chemistry, in biology or psychology, we find that isolation is impossible and that relation is everything."

And the manner of relatedness is determinative also. For instance, carbon atoms related in one way become charcoal. But carbon atoms in another relation become diamond. We human beings are part of this same creation. Our life as humans depends on our relatedness, and the manner of our relating determines the results of that relationship.

When the Bible commands "Thou shalt love" if you expect to live in any humanly significant way, it speaks the truth for all of us. For the relationship of love is the truly creative relationship. In the relation of love, new souls are born. In relations of love, a home comes into being. In the relationship of love, by which is meant not emotion only, but acting in the best interests of others, cities grow and survive, schools are built and staffed, hospitals rise to heal the sick, nations develop governments respecting the rights of the individual citizen. Love creates in human relations, hatred destroys. In short, love is the native habitat of the human being. He dies without it.

In a little book written by Dr. Smiley Blanton entitled *Love or Perish*, this truth is demonstrated in a way that is convincing, if heartbreaking. He tells the story of an orphanage located in one of the South American countries. To this place were brought abandoned babies or orphans of a parent who had died. The orphanage was short-handed, and while the Sisters did their best, they had time for little else than the daily feeding and bathing of these children. There was little or no time to cuddle them, to rock them, to play with them, to talk with them and teach them to talk. Physically, their every need was provided, but a child is more than a puppy or a kitten. A part of his being is not nourished by milk or cereal. A part of his being thrives *only on love*.

There were ninety-five babies in this orphanage, ranging in age from three months to three years. Within three months of admission, signs of abnormality began to appear. The children lost their appetites, they couldn't sleep. Their eyes began to reveal only the mournful expression of vacancy. By the end of five months, the rate of deterioration had accelerated. Most of the babies began to be shrunken and distorted in feature, so as hardly to resemble babies. They lay in their cribs whimpering. When picked up by a doctor or nurse they would shrink back in fright or strike back in fear, and in another moment cling in panic to the adult. Before they were removed to other quarters, twenty-seven of the ninety-five had died. Seven more died in the second year of their life. Twenty-five more survived but had deteriorated to the point where they had to be classified as hopeless neurotics. The human being can't live without love in some degree. I have a booklet in my library with this title, "You Can't Be Human Alone." And the truth is, you can't.

Our faith teaches us that Jesus came to seek and to save those who are lost. What does it mean to be lost? It means, doesn't it, to be "out of contact," unable to establish contact with other human beings. It is a startling fact that in this day of material affluence, in this day when we know more about our physical ailments than ever before, in this day when we send men and women into orbit about the Earth and hope to reach the moon, that there are millions of people who have never learned how to bridge the gap between themselves and another, and are in fact "out of contact," lost.

And largely because of this, I am sure, emotional illness is becoming our number one health problem. One out of every nine persons you know will sometime, before his death, find his way to a doctor seeking help for emotional sickness. What must any one of us do to inherit life, life with anything more than animal satisfactions? The answer is "Thou shalt love." Note here that *love* is an active verb. The word isn't "Thou shalt be loved." This is the result, not the cause. *What Christ is saying is that if we really want to live, we had better begin to find* some *way to express* some *love for* some*body.* This kind of love, this Divine love if you will, reaches out to someone, to anyone, in fact, whom we can help.

Maybe all you can do is to tell someone you love him. That's a start. But you'll be happier and healthier in spirit if you act out your love for your neighbor. *And who is your neighbor? Anyone who needs you for any reason.*

Yes, it is the nature of the human being that he must live in relationships to be human, to really live. *And love, active goodwill, is the little locksmith that picks the lock to every door behind which a lonely, and oftentimes rebellious, spirit is imprisoned.*

Try acting out the meaning of love to somebody today, will you? If you do, you will discover what it really means to live. You will discover that LIFE spelled in capital letters does not consist primarily in what we eat, or what we drink or how we are clothed. Life of man consists in loving, loving God, loving ourselves properly and loving our neighbors as ourselves.

And you will be surprised, if you really look for opportunities to express goodwill or love to your neighbor, how much more real God will become to you, and also how much more easily you can love yourself. And that, too, is important.

This becomes life lived as any human life must be lived, in creative relationships with others, in confident faith that God is the ground of our human life, and with such esteem and respect for oneself that our days and nights are not spent in self-loathing guilt. What must we do to really live? Learn to love God, yourself and your fellow man. And the best place to begin is with your fellow man. I dare you to try it, today. Thou shalt love… This is God's gentle command.

Hope Springs Eternal

February 28, 1965

"But now we see not yet all things put under him. But we see Jesus..."
Hebrews 2: 8-9 (KJV)

"Hope springs eternal in the human breast." So wrote Alexander Pope in "An Essay on Man." This God-given quality in human life, which keeps man forever reaching out and up, believing in the future, and working for what he believes, has brought us along our pilgrimage from savagery to civilization. Hope is the "atomic energy" of the human soul. It is the incentive which releases the creative power in man and replenishes it when man grows weary of trying.

But what happens when hope dies? Effort ceases, progress is halted, decay sets in, be it in individual man or society. And hope can die. This may lead to suicide, more often to surrender to circumstance. Coleridge diagnosed the death of hope in these lines. "Work without hope draws nectar in a sieve. And hope without an object cannot live." So, he who can inspire hope in the individual man, in a generation of men, becomes one of the saving factors in his life. This, I insist, is the contribution of true Christianity to mankind. Christ is the ground of our hope, and, as we confess in our creed, "the promise of our deliverance from sin and death."

The object of our hope, according to the Christian ideal, is in the prayer "Thy Kingdom come, thy will be done on earth as it is in heaven." But I remind you, the prayer is only the beginning, the definition of our hope. "A good world is an achievement, not a gift. The values of God, to be actual, must be woven into the warp and woof of the organized life of the world," said Dr. Eustace Haydon some years ago.

Some biblical literalists prefer the vision of John, as related in the Book of Revelation, who saw "... the holy city, new Jerusalem, coming down from God out of heaven..." It appeals, perhaps, because it seems to relieve us of any responsibility for its becoming. This "let God do it" attitude of some Christians has no doubt contributed to the growth of the secular mind in America, a mind which has lost faith in the church and hope that it is capable of making much difference in the real world of human relations. Preoccupied with organization, dogma, ritual and church buildings (and all are important, though not ALL-important), we have let the world of men get along as best it can. So, the magnitude of our world crisis seen against the history of the church as representing Christ, may indeed create a big question mark in many minds. *Yet, I insist that the Christian faith is still the soil in which hope is cultivated, and the Christian objective one to inspire our unrelenting efforts.*

Let us look again at the reasons for our hope. We stand where some first century Christians stood, when looking out upon their world, assessing their situation. Reaching back into the Psalms, their library of religious inspiration, they were reminded of God's purpose and creation of man, making him but "a little lower than the angels, and hast crowned him with glory and honor. ... Thou has put all things under his feet." Yet, in all honesty, they admitted failure and long-delayed realization.

Undismayed, they went on to affirm, "But now we see not yet all things put under him. But we see Jesus ..." And that last phrase is the difference between hope and despair. And that same phrase can lift us out of despondence over a world in grave trouble, giving us, too, a rebirth of hope. The Christian lives by three great resources, all of them rooted in the Eternal God Himself. They are the resources of Faith, Hope and Love. And you will notice that Hope is bracketed between Faith and Love. The Christian stands in the position of hope because he has his feet firmly grounded in a great faith and a dynamic love. *And he stands on these two pillars of faith and love because they have been historically proven to be dependable.* "Experience produces hope" when that experience has tested these two resources, Faith and Love.

On one side of hope there is Faith, faith in God. And the Christian faith asserts that God, the Eternal source of life and being, is disclosed to our understanding in the life and person of Jesus Christ. Christ is to us a window through which we can look to see how God works with and for mankind. And, believing what we see, we believe that the Eternal purpose and power is devoted to our good, to our enlightenment through discovery of truth, to our enrichment through discovery of the beautiful and the true, into our maturing as men and women after the pattern of Christ.

For having discovered a clue to the nature of the human in Christ Jesus, we find our faith in mankind renewed as well. If we should spend all our time studying the "rogues gallery" of the human race, we might well despair of mankind. But only a fool would do that. The roster of the human family includes so much that is great and good and creative that we cannot despair of man, and particularly since we have come to know the Man Jesus Christ. And the more we know of the human race, we discover in it reason for a renewed faith in man.

James Michener, distinguished author, has this to say in a statement he titled, "All Men are My Brothers," part of the *This I Believe* radio series. "I really believe that every man on this earth is my brother," in other words, capable of relating to him in a helpful, mutually beneficial way. He then goes on to document this statement from his experiences among people of all the races. In India, Japan, the New Hebrides, the Islands of the Sea, beyond even the barriers of language, he found men like himself, hosts to the same hungers, fears, hopes, needs. "*I really believe every man on this earth is my brother,*" said he. "*He has a soul like mine, the ability to understand friendship, the capacity to create beauty. In all the continents of this world I have met such men.*"

Commenting on the cultural differences which seem to separate men, he recounted how, in the New Hebrides, the Lennaneans ate roast dog while he ate Army Spam, each no doubt thinking the other strange, if not actually balmy.

He discovered the Golden Rule of Christ to be just that, pure gold, because it is the secret of finding in another man the man you are yourself. So Jesus, in giving the Golden Rule, is saying, "I can treat others as I would be treated because they share my same needs and hopes and fears and hungers and possibilities." And who can ever despair of man when he sees him through the eyes of Jesus Christ? Yes, we stand in a posture of hope, because we stand on a great faith in God as eternal love, and in man, as capable of greatness, greatness glimpsed in Jesus Christ.

But the other side of hope is LOVE, as action. And here again, experience with love, as a way of life, becomes the ground of our hope. Having seen Jesus, we cannot doubt the power of love to transform human individuals and human society. The story of His life on earth, His transformation of the "Sons of Thunder," James and John, into the apostles of peace, His infusion of stability in the flabbiness of Simon, until he was called "Peter the Rock." We cannot forget Matthew, the materialist, tax-gatherer and lover of money, recreated into an evangelist by his fellowship with Christ. Nor can we overlook Saul, the persecutor of innocent men or women, even to executing the death sentence, becoming one who could live and then write that great ode to love in Chapter 13 of the Corinthian letter.

But it did not stop there; for these nineteen centuries, this man Jesus, through whom we get a glimpse of the Eternal God, has, by the power of Love, emancipated women from virtual slavery and given childhood a place of highest honor in the family of men. This same spirit has changed tyranny into democracy, slavery into freedom. Through this spirit schools are open to all alike, and hospitals wait with open door for the sick to be healed. And through the example of his own victory over death, Christ has invested millions upon millions with the comfort of an eternal hope as they approach the end of this life. The hold of Christ upon the world has been and still is the hold of love upon the conscience and the imagination of the human race.

See how it works in human situations. Lt. Howard DeLong was given charge of a prisoner of war camp in the Philippine Islands during the war. Now, one would hardly consider this to be an ideal situation for the development of tender sentiments among men. But DeLong was a Christian, trained as a young man to have respect for the human being. Though in charge of their camp, he never ceased to show concern for them as persons. He made sure they were well fed and clothed and housed. He worked out things for them to do to make time meaningful for them. He did all possible to keep up their morale. The time came for the camp to be evacuated, and some of the men presented him with a plaque, an engraved stone, no less, with these words, "The righteous shall be held in everlasting remembrance."

Or consider the case of Floyd Schmoe, a Quaker by faith, a teacher of forestry at the University of Washington. He believed, as a Quaker, that there is "that of God in every man." Speaking about his reaction to the terrible bombings which were part of the war effort of our own country, as well as that of our enemies, he said, "After Hiroshima I felt fear for a civilization fallen so low, a pained conscience, that I, and all who had failed in our efforts to find a better way, shared responsibility for this unspeakable crime."

But, you say, these people were our enemies. Yes, but they were also God's children and members of the family of mankind. *Unable to be at peace with himself, this good man with some friends returned to Nagasaki, Japan, the other city bombed with atomic missiles, and built twenty-nine homes, two community halls, and a laundry for those completely dispossessed people. You see, this is what love is like.* It does this to people and with people. And it has the power to awaken response in kind.

After the First World War, the Quakers went into Germany to assist in the distribution of food to the starving victims of war (and, incidentally, provided in great amount by the compassion of the American people) under the direction of the late Herbert Hoover. During a particularly severe typhoid epidemic, one of the young social workers died. It so happened that she had been working in a village which was for the most part Catholic in its religious life.

The death necessitated a burial, of course, and the only cemetery was the Catholic burial ground. Since she was not Catholic, her body could not lie in consecrated soil. But the kindly people dug a grave as close to the fence which enclosed the cemetery as possible and attended in large number the simple funeral given her. The grave was filled, and the folk returned to their homes. But that was not the end of the story. *During the night some folk, we will likely never know who, opened the fence and, stretching it out, moved it to enclose the grave of this apostle of love, within the sacred place.* Those who had been the objects of her love did not wish to be separated from her even in death.

Yes, faith in God and Man, God as Eternal Love and Man as one family with capacity to reach the stature of man as seen in Christ, is a foundation stone of our hope. And across from Faith is Love, God in action through man, transforming foes into friends, providing the gentle cohesion which has power to bind this broken world; we see Jesus, and so, we are apostles of undying hope.

THOUGHTS ON COLLECTION FIVE

Those final three messages speak volumes to me. Tackling first a really difficult emotion to talk about in *The Guilt That Haunts Us*, Grandpa breaks through with a message focused on the incredible discomfort we all feel at times, some of us much more frequently than others.

Perhaps even ahead of his time, he even mentions "white guilt," but doesn't leave it there. He dives straight into the guilt of existence of any and all "pigmented" peoples. In fact, what followed those observances was something interesting. Grandpa conflates our humanity as a conflict between our "animal" and "spiritual" existence into one large melting pot of struggle. This is one of my favorite quotes from the book:

> "Perhaps by our very *humanity*, the fact that we are both animal and spirit, that we live in the tension of a dual being with the necessity of making ethical judgments by our nature, we are often under a sense of general condemnation."

We all fall short of the Glory of God. Pretty simple. I really like it. Regardless of who we are or what we look like on the outside. We're all human. We all feel this way.

Squaring that fact of humanity up with each other, *all* others, is perhaps one way we can actually celebrate our equality, instead of focusing on our diversity.

Could that idea lead to a brighter future where we can finally see we're more *alike* than we are different?

Maybe aligning our sight lines to that idea and working through this tension-filled life with our eyes fixed on Christ, maybe there we can build a "Church of Our Dreams."

If you haven't yet had time to read Latasha Morrison's, *Be the Bridge*, I would recommend it.

Grandpa then comes at us with *God Commands – But Gently*. It paints a beautiful, futuristic picture of what loving our neighbor really looks like. It also hits on something we are talking more and more about today – the state of our mental health.

Think about this passage, from 1963!

> "And largely because of this, I am sure, emotional illness is becoming our number one health problem. One out of every nine persons you know will sometime, before his death, find his way to a doctor seeking help for emotional sickness."

Boom. There it is. The plague of 2022.

The cure? Relational and Intentional Love in action for a Neighbor, defined as ANYONE who needs you for any reason.

Another haymaker:

> "And love, active goodwill, is the little locksmith that picks the lock to every door behind which a lonely, and oftentimes rebellious, spirit is imprisoned."

Amen. That's where joy lives, dear reader.

Right. There.

Because Christianity demonstrates our private guilt can be made better through our pursuit of loving our public neighbor, we truly can believe that *Hope Springs Eternal*. Grandpa really did a number on me when he showed how sandwiching Hope between Faith and Love can prove to be dependable. We can count on the next sixty years being better than the previous times if we will choose to experience the reliable, trusted result of interweaving our Faith in God and Love for Neighbors into our daily interactions.

The results, and I have seen them, will no doubt give you Hope in the human existence. We can begin to say goodbye to Greed, Selfishness, Personal Ambition, Hatred, Disdain, Frustration, Adultery and all the other ugly traits.

It really does work. *We* simply must believe it will and then decide it's worth it to try.

Jump off the board into the deep end.

Give the world the Heisman. Be Bold. Choose Intentional Love. Learn the History, it helps answer so many questions, and then Lean Hard into the Future following what you learn.

I honestly believe you'll like what you find. It'll be hard work, no doubt.

And, you may still need a Coors Light after a long day.

I still do.

That's OK. Jesus' first miracle was turning water into wine.

Baby steps at first. But trust me, Joy awaits those who will try. Real Joy. Unfiltered Joy.

Final Thoughts

Just a quick caveat. I do *not* have it all figured out. I am in continuous thought, inspired by some impactful material. I spend several hours a week reading, listening to podcasts, engaging in documentaries on history and more. I find my mind craves the stuff, like homemade chocolate chip cookies, I mean really good ones. I try to eat just two… but it quickly turns to seven. That's what it's like when I get into a good book, especially one engaging my faith.

In *Backpacking in a Cultural Wilderness*, I discovered something that helped me see the bigger picture, through my grandfather's eyes. In some ways, many ways, I am not qualified to comment on anything C. Maxwell Brown said in any of the messages enclosed in this book; to even think I could have something to say about them gives me pause.

In other ways, I may be one of the most qualified. Why? I believe my grandfather was writing to people just like me. People who have been on the fence about God. People who really need to think deeply about what to do about Him. People who love their families, their communities and attend church, but are still yearning to connect to something a little deeper, even more fulfilling.

Grandpa Max wanted to touch that nerve in all our consciences that releases "God's Vibrations" into our bodies and minds, and when they're the "good, good, good vibrations," we naturally want to invite others to experience them.

In reading these messages, these short stories, I was struck with just how relatable much of their content is. Again, these messages are nearly sixty years old, and yet the conditions we find ourselves in today are unbelievably similar.

It's almost eerie.

They leave me wondering about the future. In some ways hopeful about it. In other ways concerned. But absolutely convicted in purpose. If we truly desire a world improved for all people, it's time to dive into the source of our potential for reconciliation with all the conditions that afflict us—those that prevent true community from being realized.

It's time to seek God. It's time to strive to be more like Jesus. It's time to actually work that out in our lives. It's time to listen. To pray. To light the fire of our collective consciences—to move forward together, equally, as children of God.

The Gospel of Luke tells the story of questioning the authority of Jesus. It goes like this:

> One day as Jesus was teaching the people in the temple courts and proclaiming the good news, the chief priests and the teachers of the law, together with the elders, came up to him. "Tell us by what authority you are doing these things," they said. "Who gave you this authority?"
>
> He replied, "I will also ask you a question. Tell me: John's baptism—was it from heaven, or of human origin?"
>
> They discussed it among themselves and said, "If we say, 'From heaven,' he will ask, 'Why didn't you believe him?' But if we say, 'Of human origin,' all the people will stone us, because they are persuaded that John was a prophet."
>
> So they answered, "We don't know where it was from."

Final Thoughts

Jesus said, "Neither will I tell you by what authority I am doing these things."

Here's where this one hits me. The chief priests know the correct answer. They knew, maybe even intrinsically, that John's baptism was from heaven. They were just too scared of the implications of admitting it.

They were afraid of the "Why didn't you believe him?" consequences. The kind of consequences that would have called their own wisdom into question. By providing the answer they knew to be true, they would have been humbled. And that, that emotion, is so hard for so many of us to manage. Imagine what would have happened if they had been bold? If they had humbled themselves before the One they had seen perform miracle after miracle and prove time and again that his knowledge of the scriptures was unparalleled.

What if they had humbled themselves in Faith, Hope and Love? His Love?

I haven't said too much in this book about being humble. But one of my life's verses can be found in 1 Peter 5:6-7 (NIV): "Humble yourselves, therefore, under God's mighty hand, that he may lift you up in due time. Cast all your anxiety on him because he cares for you."

I just love that one.

Here's another saying I love about being humble that comes from someone, ironically of the same name. Peter Kerridge is the CEO of Premier Christian Communications in London and a new friend of mine. He shared this thought with me earlier this year, and man, it rings true:

"You'll be amazed at what God can do, as long as you don't want the Glory."

Amen?

Thank you for taking your time to read this book.

May God bless you and yours.

"Walk away from anger, walk away from pain, walk away from anguish, walk into the rain." From "Dead Man's Rope" by Sting.

What Feeds My Brain?

In the event you've got an itch to take your walk just a little deeper, and I hope and pray you do, here are some resources I have found that provide me with enrichment, and they push me a little bit, too.

Books I Have Enjoyed

The Bible

Dominion - Tom Holland

Love Has a Name - Adam Weber

UnBelievable? - Justin Brierley

Everything Happens for a Reason - Kate Bowler

A Little History of the World - E.H. Gombrich

Bullies and Saints - John Dickson

Be The Bridge - Latasha Morrison

A Greater Story - Sam Collier

The Fate of The Apostles - Sean McDowell

Why Trust the Bible? - Amy Orr-Ewing

Cry Like a Man - Jason Wilson

Live to Forgive - Jason Romano

Emotionally Healthy Spirituality - Peter Scazzero

Tuesdays With Morrie - Mitch Albom

The Richest Man in Town - V.J. Smith

Backpacking In a Cultural Wilderness - C. Maxwell Brown

The Air We Breathe - Glen Scrivener

Podcasts I Regularly Enjoy

Undeceptions - John Dickson

UnBelievable? - Justin Brierley

The Conversation - Adam Weber

ResGen Giving Life Podcast - Tom Henderson

Rise & Fall of Mars Hill - Christianity Today

ManDate - Ben Krush and Ryan Konz

Books Up Next

Battle Cry - Jason Wilson

Growing Slow - Jennifer Dukes Lee

God's Forever Family - Larry Eskridge

Let The World See - Sam Acho

The Hole in Our Gospel - Richard Stearns

A Doubter's Guide to World Religions - John Dickson

Do No Harm - Henry Marsh

Endnotes

About Grandpa's Gift (Dan)

1. Lyrics.com, STANDS4 LLC, 2022. "Everything Old Is New Again Lyrics." Accessed November 10, 2022. https://www.lyrics.com/lyric/403272/Peter+Allen/Everything+Old+Is+New+Again

For the Loneliness that Desolates Us

2. Santayana, George. "To W. P." Accessed November 10, 2022. https://www.poetryfoundation.org/poems/46002/to-w-p

For the Joys that Invite Us

3. Christianity.com, "Bishops Ridley and Latimer Burned." Accessed November 10, 2022, https://www.christianity.com/church/church-history/timeline/1501-1600/bishops-ridley-and-latimer-burned-11629990.html

You Can Find God in History

4. Quotefancy.com, "Top 500 Leo Tolstoy Quotes (2022 Update)." Accessed November 10, 2022, https://quotefancy.com/quote/851846
5. Christianity Today online; "Dr. Paul Carlson: A Life at Stake." Accessed November 10, 2022, https://www.christianitytoday.com/ct/1964/december-4/church-and-state-dr-paul-carlson-life-at-stake.html
6. Shakespeare, William. Macbeth. Act 5, Scene 5. Accessed November 10, 2022, https://shakespeare.folger.edu/shakespeares-works/macbeth/entire-play/

The God Who Intervenes

7. Marquis, Don. "The Young Moses." Poetrynook.com, Accessed November 10, 2022, https://www.poetrynook.com/poem/young-moses
8. Schaff, Philip. Person of Christ: The Miracle of History. With a Reply to Strauss and Renan, and a Collection of Testimonies of Unbelievers. "How Did the Life of Jesus Impact the World?" Christian Classics Ethereal Library online, Accessed November 10, 2022, https://ccel.org/home3/search?text=Philip+Schaff%2C+Person+of+Christ%3A+The+Miracle+of+History.+With+a+Reply+to+ Strauss+and+Renan%2C+and+a+Collection+of+Testimonies+of+Unbelievers&genreID=&orderBy=Relevance

Endnotes

For The Guilt That Haunts Us

9. Anglican Orthodox Church International website; "The General Confession of the Book of Common Prayer," Accessed November 10, 2022, https://aocinternational.org/the-general-confession-of-the-book-of-common-prayer/
10. Shakespeare, William. Othello. Act 5, Scene 1. Accessed November 10, 2022, https://shakespeare.folger.edu/shakespeares-works/othello/

ABOUT THE AUTHOR

Dan LaRock is first a Believer, husband, father and son.

He is also an entrepreneur, an executive shareholder with HUB International - Great Plains, a co-founder of Rock Ranch, a frequent communicator and speaker and deeply and experienced in public relations and institutional advancement. Dan is currently the national Nonprofit Specialty Practice Leader for Employee Benefits for HUB International. He has been blessed to work with entrepreneurial leaders at incredible companies from across the Upper Midwest including Iowa, Minnesota, Nebraska, North Dakota, South Dakota and Wisconsin.

He is a current board member for Premier Insight, The University of Sioux Falls and Southwest Minnesota CEO. He also serves on steering committees for Children's Home Society of South Dakota, Sioux Valley

Energy and *The Mandate Podcast*. He is a worship leader for various churches in SW Minnesota, NW Iowa and SE South Dakota. He is a former school board member for Hills – Beaver Creek ISD #671 in Minnesota.

Dan and his family reside in Sioux Falls, South Dakota.

For speaking engagements, bulk book orders and more information, please visit: www.grandpasgiftbook.com